BATTLE READY

BOLD MEN OF GOD SERIES
JOSHUA · CALEB

BATTLE READY

PREPARE TO BE USED BY GOD

STEVE
FARRAR

David C Cook®

transforming lives together

BATTLE READY
Published by David C Cook
4050 Lee Vance View
Colorado Springs, CO 80918 U.S.A.

David C Cook Distribution Canada
55 Woodslee Avenue, Paris, Ontario, Canada N3L 3E5

David C Cook U.K., Kingsway Communications
Eastbourne, East Sussex BN23 6NT, England

The graphic circle C logo is a registered trademark of David C Cook.

Unless otherwise noted, all Scripture quotations are taken from *The Holy Bible, English Standard Version*. Copyright © 2000; 2001 by Crossway Bibles, a division of Good News Publishers. Used by permission. All rights reserved. Scripture quotations marked NASB are taken from the *New American Standard Bible*, © Copyright 1960, 1995 by The Lockman Foundation. Used by permission; KJV are taken from the King James Version of the Bible. (Public Domain); NKJV are taken from the New King James Version. Copyright © 1982 by Thomas Nelson, Inc. Used by permission. All rights reserved; PH are taken from J. B. Phillips: *The New Testament in Modern English*, revised editions © J. B. Phillips, 1958, 1960, 1972, permission of Macmillan Publishing Co. and Collins Publishers; MSG are taken from *THE MESSAGE*. Copyright © by Eugene H. Peterson 1993, 1994, 1995, 1996, 2000, 2001, 2002. Used by permission of NavPress Publishing Group; and NIV are taken from the *Holy Bible, New International Version®. NIV®.* Copyright © 1973, 1978, 1984 International Bible Society. Used by permission of Zondervan. All rights reserved. The author has added italics to Scripture quotations for emphasis.

LCCN 2009929672
ISBN 978-1-4347-6869-8
eISBN 978-0-7814-0349-8

© 2009 Steve Farrar
Published in association with the literary agency of WordServe Literary
Group, Ltd., 10152 S. Knoll Circle, Highlands Ranch, CO 80130

The Team: Don Pape, Larry Libby, Amy Kiechlin,
Sarah Schultz, Jack Campbell, and Karen Athen
Cover Design: Nick Lee

Printed in the United States of America
First Edition 2009

7 8 9 10 11

012314

To
Ken Sibley
and
Willie Hornberger
In appreciation for their stellar friendship

Contents

Acknowledgments 9

1. Hard Times 11

2. Giants 31

3. Gravitas 55

4. Slaves 77

5. Increased Hardship 99

6. Circling the Airport 121

7. High Wire Promotion 145

8. The Worst Possible Time 165

9. Fighting Off Fear 183

10. Three Tasks 205

11. Two Spies 225

12. God Is My Banker 245

Study Questions for Personal Reflection or Small-Group Discussion 255

Notes 279

Acknowledgments

Good friends are hard to come by. I am especially grateful that I get to publish with some of my best friends. To work with Dan Rich and Don Pape at David C. Cook is a flat-out pleasure. These guys are absolute pros, and working with men of their caliber and character makes the entire process nothing less than a first-class experience. Larry Libby is another guy who can make the sometimes-grueling experience of writing a joy. What an editor and what a friend. This is our ninth book together—I hope we get to do nine more. And a special thanks to Jack Campbell for his excellent work in the often underappreciated task of copyediting. His eagle eye saved me much grief!

Chapter One

Hard Times

"I was born for a storm and a calm does not suit me."
—Andrew Jackson

T hese are the times that try men's souls."

Thomas Paine penned those words in 1776 in a pamphlet he titled "Crisis."

It was an appropriate title for his day. The young American colonies certainly faced a great crisis, feeling the oppressive weight of the English king and his invading army. Men who spoke out for freedom found themselves in serious danger.

Take Joseph Warren, for example. Gathering his courage, he dared to speak out about the situation his country was in. And for so doing, he was beheaded by British officers at Bunker Hill, who then presented his head to their commanding general.[1]

I am writing these words on December 1, 2008. Never in my fifty-nine years on this earth have I seen so many men so deeply troubled. It is accurate to say once again, "These are the times that try men's souls."

Joshua and Caleb, two heroes from the pages of the Bible, will figure prominently in this book. But I'm not going to start with Joshua and Caleb. I'm going to begin with Samuel Adams and John Hancock.

Contrary to popular opinion, Samuel Adams did not run a brewery. And John Hancock did not sell life insurance.

These men were both friends of Joseph Warren, and like Warren, they were not afraid to speak out against tyranny. They knew very well that they could be beheaded just as Warren had been. But that fact did not curb their tongues or their pens. In fact, when the British general Thomas Gage attempted to quell the revolution and offered amnesty to every man in the colonies who would lay down his weapon, two men, and two men only, were excluded from the offer of amnesty and forgiveness. Those two men were Samuel Adams and John Hancock. These two bold leaders would not be forgiven under any circumstances—so great was their opposition to the king and their influence in the colonies.

Samuel Adams was the most popular columnist in all of New England, and John Hancock may have been the wealthiest man in all of Massachusetts. Though differing widely in personality and style, these men had something profound in common that formed the bedrock of their friendship: They were deeply committed to Jesus Christ and His inspired Word. That's what made them the Joshua and Caleb of their generation. They were absolutely fearless in the face of a giant invading army and the world's largest navy. But the foundation of their courage was their hope and trust in the God of Abraham, Isaac, and Jacob. He was their Father, their Foundation, and their Hope.

Even as other men wilted under pressure and feared for their very lives, Adams and Hancock stood firm. Don't imagine it was an easy thing to do; it's never easy to hold the line when you live in soul-trying times.

Our Times

In the course of my ministry, I have had the privilege of speaking to men all across the country. And it's very clear to me as I interact with men that once again "these are the times that try men's souls."

If there is a verse that speaks to the condition of men in our day and time, I believe it is Psalm 42:5 (NASB):

Why are you in despair [sunk down], O my soul?
And why have you become disturbed within me?
Hope in God, for I shall again praise Him
For the help of His presence [saving acts].

Everywhere across our land, men are discouraged and depressed—and some verging on outright despair. So let's answer the question of the psalmist. Notice that he is talking to himself instead of listening to himself. When we are panicked and fearful, we are listening to ourselves—listening to the killing worries and anxieties that fuel our negative imaginations like a windblown forest fire. The psalmist, however, attempting to fight off the fear that has become epidemic in his heart and mind, *speaks* to himself instead of listening to himself.

In the process, he asks himself a significant question:

"Why are you in despair, O my soul?"

If most men today were to answer that question, I believe their answer would center in a fearful giant named "Uncertainty." This giant, of course, has been around since the beginning of time, sometimes more visible and sometimes less. In recent days, however, it has been stalking our land with a vengeance. Why? Because ...

- there is giant uncertainty over the meltdown of the economy; and
- there is giant uncertainty over the breakdown of the nation.

The Meltdown of the Economy

It's difficult to pick up a newspaper or news magazine without getting hints about the possibility of another Great Depression. For nearly a decade, we had a remarkable run of prosperity and economic growth. Jobs have been plentiful, salaries rising, and people have had the time and leisure to travel and indulge in a delicious assortment of personal luxuries.

But then in a matter of months, everything began to fall apart.

Gigantic financial institutions and banks began to collapse, and people began to panic. The real-estate market across the nation began to nose-dive, and once-staid-and-stable firms began to issue pinks slips like candy. One headline from the September 18, 2008, edition of the *Wall Street Journal* sums it all up: *Worst Crisis Since '30s, With No End Yet in Sight*.[2]

The prosperity and financial growth had all seemed so certain. But we have come to realize that it was an illusion. Of course, we should have known that all along. Note the words of 1 Timothy 6:17 (NASB): "Instruct those who are rich in this present world not to be conceited or to fix their hope on the uncertainty of riches, but on God, who richly supplies us with all things to enjoy."

Did you catch that? Those who are rich in this present world (and that would be the vast majority of Americans compared to the rest of the world) *are not to fix their hope on the uncertainty of riches*.

Quite frankly, most of us have been living as though the riches were certain—living as though the prosperity wouldn't end, as though real estate would keep going up forever, as though our jobs would always be secure. The average American felt like he was bulletproof when it came to his prosperity. And this is why so many are now depressed and in despair. Now, many who were close to retirement will never see retirement. They have simply lost too much in the market, and there's just not enough time to make it all back.

The Breakdown of the Nation

There is a sense in this country that things are spiraling out of control, not just economically but also politically and socially. You can feel the tremors, as the foundations of American law and government are being shaken to the core. This includes a raging current of anti-Christian bias flowing through our courts, universities, and media.

In the recent economic bailout, fundamental principles of democracy and commerce were thrown away in a matter of days. It was all done out of panic and fear. And once the government gets more power, it is not prone to give it back at a later date. What it takes—it keeps.

And that changes everything.

Back in the 1970s, I remember hearing the great Christian thinker Francis Schaeffer talk about the direction that America was headed. Schaeffer said he believed America would eventually wind up as a dictatorship, and he wasn't sure if it would come from the right or the left. It was Schaeffer's opinion that some great calamity and crisis would threaten the well-being of the average American. It would be of such a magnitude that people would willingly give up their rights if they could be promised just two things: personal peace and affluence. And if personal peace and affluence would be guaranteed, they would immediately accept an elite dictator who would sweep away their blood-bought freedoms without a second thought. Perhaps we are not too far from that scenario—or perhaps that scenario won't occur at all. No one on this side of heaven knows for sure.

But there is no question that we are in deep decline. You have heard of the rise and fall of great nations. We know in our hearts that we are not only falling—we are free-falling. And nobody seems to have a parachute.

In my previous book, *God Built*, I referred to the work of Sir John Glubb. In 1976, he wrote an essay titled "The Fate of Empires." Glubb put forth his theory that great empires rarely survive more than 250 years.[3]

The Nation	Dates	Time in Years
Assyria	859–612 BC	247
Persia	538–330 BC	208
Greece	331–100 BC	231
Roman Republic	260–27 BC	233
Roman Empire	27 BC–AD 180	207
Arab Empire	AD 634–880	246
Mameluke Empire	AD 1250–1517	267
Ottoman Empire	AD 1320–1570	250
Spain	AD 1500–1750	250
Romanov Russia	AD 1682–1916	234
Britain	AD 1700–1950	250[4]

We are not so concerned for ourselves as we are for our children and grandchildren. They are living in an America that is a far cry from the one that previous generations knew.

So this is why so many men in America who look at life through the lens of Scripture and history are fighting off depression and despair. When one looks at the economic meltdown along with the national breakdown, one sees we are facing a future that is nothing short of a gigantic uncertainty.

Is there any hope?

Yes, there is.

And it's right in the text of Psalm 42:5 (NASB):

> Why are you in despair [sunk down], O my soul?
>> And why have you become disturbed within me?
> Hope in God, for I shall again praise Him
>> For the help of His presence [saving acts].

Triple Shot of Hope

As the psalmist continues to talk himself out of depression, he reminds himself about God. Because God exists and because of His great attributes, the psalmist tells himself that he will again praise God for the help of His presence. And when God is present, He saves His people. All is not lost—God is in absolute control.

The source of our depression these days is gigantic uncertainty about the economy and the future of the nation. But there are three certainties that form the (true) foundation of our hope:

- The certainty of providence
- The certainty of the promises
- The certainty of the plan

In our times of giant uncertainty about the economy and our nation, those three certainties are nothing less than a triple shot—not of espresso, but of hope.

The Certainty of Providence

The providence of God simply means that God will provide; He will give you what you need when you need it. He will sustain you and keep you going. Ron Mehl used to say that God worked the night shift. What he meant by that was that grocery stores restock every twenty-four hours, and that restock takes place during the night shift. If you walk into a grocery store at two in the morning, it looks like mass chaos. Boxes litter the aisles, and employees run here and there, working feverishly to put product on the shelves. All of this goes on when 98 percent of the neighborhood is asleep. So even while you're sleeping, someone is working to restock the store so that whatever you need in the morning will be there. Maybe at 9:30 p.m. aisle 12 was out of raisins. But at 7:00 the next morning the shelves on aisle 12 will be loaded with raisin boxes, all in neat order in a fully synchronized display. The raisins are ready and waiting before you ever need them.[5]

God works the night shift and the day shift. He never sleeps. His eye is constantly upon you. He knows everything about you. He knows your worries, your pressures, and how much money (to the penny) that you will need to survive until the moment you die. And He will provide that money at exactly the right time.

Let me give you a verse that will Advil your anxiety.

Psalm 103:19 (NASB) states that …

> The LORD has established His throne in the heavens,
> And His sovereignty rules over all.

Now who sits on a throne? A king sits on a throne. God is King over everything—no exceptions. This great God is King who sits in the heavens, and His sovereignty rules over all. What is sovereignty? Sovereignty is control. Control of what?

Everything.

He's in control of everything—even evil. He's never the author of evil because His character is holy—absolutely pure and flawless. But He *controls* evil and *uses* evil for His purposes—for the good of His people and the glory of His name. I know that's a stretch to think about, but the Bible strongly declares that He is in control of all things—*including* evil. Solomon put it like this:

> The LORD has made everything for its own purpose,
> Even the wicked for the day of evil. (Prov. 16:4 NASB)

How can God do that and still be good? I don't know, and I can't explain it. I can't begin to understand how that works, and neither can you. But that is what the Bible teaches. Psalm 119:68 says that *the Lord is good and does good.* So this good and great God is the King of the entire world and all of the universes. He spoke them all into existence. He created them, and He owns them. And catch this—*He keeps them going.* He sustains everything within His creation and keeps it all together. Hebrews 1:3 (NASB) states that the Lord Jesus continuously "upholds all things by the word of His power." That means He keeps it all going—including you and your family, regardless of the strength of the economy.

He is your King and He is your Banker. His providence will keep you provisioned and sustained.

The Heidelberg Catechism was compiled in 1563. A catechism is simply a summary of the teaching of Scripture on a particular question. A catechism asks a question and then provides the biblical answer. And the section on providence is crystal clear:

> *Question 27. What dost thou mean by the providence of God?*

Answer: The almighty and everywhere present power of God; whereby, as it were by his hand, he upholds and governs heaven, earth, and all creatures; so that herbs and grass, rain and drought, fruitful and barren years, meat and drink, health and sickness, riches and poverty, yea, and all things come, not by chance, but by his fatherly hand.

Question 28. What advantage is it to us to know that God has created, and by his providence does still uphold all things?

Answer: That we may be patient in adversity; thankful in prosperity; and that in all things, which may hereafter befall us, we place our firm trust in our faithful God and Father, that nothing shall separate us from his love; since all creatures are so in his hand, that without his will they cannot so much as move.[6]

In a nutshell, that's what the Bible teaches about the providence of God.

He's in control of everything from the watermelon crop in south Texas to the price of gas in Omaha. Good economies and bad economies are under His control—along with everything else inside and outside the universe.

So let's go back to the giant uncertainties we face—the frightening meltdown of the economy and the ongoing breakdown of our beloved nation. Is our great God in control of all of these things? Yes. Will He take care of us and our families regardless of what occurs? Yes. And how do we know that? Because of His promises—and He is the God who cannot lie. Therefore, His promises are certain. And we have hope as we face the future.

The Certainty of the Promises

In Matthew 6:25, the Lord Jesus gave a staggering command:

Don't worry about your life.

The problem is, most of us live as though He never said any such thing. We *do* worry about our lives; we worry all the time.

So what are we going to do with these words of the Lord Jesus? *"Don't worry."* What does He mean by that? Does He mean we're never even to take note of and consider what's transpiring around us? Does He mean that thinking ahead and planning wisely don't really matter?

No. That's not what He means. What He does mean is that we shouldn't worry ourselves sick over what might happen. Why not? Because He has made some promises to us, and He wants us to take them seriously. He wants us to believe those promises so that we don't become overwhelmed.

The promises and the providence of God are the keys to mental health. Without them, you have no hope. But when we live off them, we are more than conquerors. My Father is watching over my life—that's why I don't have to worry about it. Now that's either true or it isn't—and if it isn't, you're in more trouble than you can comprehend. But it *is* true. He's your Father, and He's your Provider.

In the Koran, there are ninety-nine different names for Allah. But not one of them can be translated as Father.[7] Matthew 6 contains thirty-four verses, and in those thirty-four verses the Lord Jesus refers to the Father twelve times.

You have a Father who is the sovereign God, in control of all things. And He has made some promises to you that His providence guarantees. Note the promise of Matthew 6:25–34 (NASB):

> For this reason I say to you, do not be worried about your
> life, as to what you will eat or what you will drink; nor

for your body, as to what you will put on. Is not life more
than food, and the body more than clothing?

Look at the birds of the air, that they do not sow, nor
reap nor gather into barns, and yet your heavenly Father
feeds them. Are you not worth much more than they?

And who of you by being worried can add a single
hour to his life?

And why are you worried about clothing? Observe
how the lilies of the field grow; they do not toil nor do
they spin, yet I say to you that not even Solomon in all his
glory clothed himself like one of these.

But if God so clothes the grass of the field, which is
alive today and tomorrow is thrown into the furnace, will
He not much more clothe you? You of little faith!

Do not worry then, saying, "What will we eat?" or
"What will we drink?" or "What will we wear for clothing?" For the Gentiles eagerly seek all these things; for your
heavenly Father knows that you need all these things.

But seek first His kingdom and His righteousness, and
all these things will be added to you.

So do not worry about tomorrow; for tomorrow will
care for itself. Each day has enough trouble of its own.

Your Father knows that you need all of these things. And He has the
power to provide all things to you at the moment you need them. This
is the promise to those who seek Him first. And it is the reason that the
Lord Jesus told us, "Don't worry about your life." Grasp this truth and
you will have massive hope instead of depression. But the moment you
forget your Father is the moment you begin the downward spiral all over
again.

The Certainty of the Plan

God has a plan for the ages. History is going somewhere. The world is under control even though it looks like things are out of control.

The last book of the Bible, Revelation, gives a fairly detailed overview of the events that will take place at the end of the age, ushering in the return of Jesus Christ. There will be a new heaven, a new earth, and a new Jerusalem. There will be a final battle at Armageddon. And there will be a charismatic leader who will unite the world and stand against the kingdom of God. Scripture calls this individual the "Antichrist."

God has revealed His plan for the ages to His prophets. One of those men was Daniel. When God revealed to Daniel what He was going to do in the last days, it made Daniel deeply alarmed in his spirit (Dan. 7:15). And the more God revealed, the more alarmed Daniel became (v. 28). As God pulled back the curtain of time and showed His servant more and more of His plan for the ages, Daniel was so overwhelmed by what he saw that he became physically ill and exhausted (8:27). At a later time, after he was given still more insight into the plan of God, he went into mourning for three weeks (10:2).

This is why so many of us are troubled. We know that God has a plan for the ages, and we have studied the prophecies. And those of us who have looked carefully into that plan can't help noting that the United States cannot be found in the last days of biblical prophecy. Yes, we're the big boys on the block right now, but apparently something happens to us that removes us as a major player. What will happen? Nobody knows for sure, because Scripture doesn't give us the details. But it's safe to say that in the rise and fall of great nations, the United States will suffer some kind of major calamity or collapse that will drastically minimize our role on the world scene. Or maybe we just die a slow death as a result of suffocating socialism. No one on earth knows for sure what is going to happen to our nation. But we do know that *something* is going to happen to drastically minimize our influence.

And when we think about these future events—and the hard times that are ahead for our nation—it makes us sick, just as Daniel was sickened by what he saw. It makes us deeply troubled.

In John 14:1–3 (NASB), the Lord Jesus spoke directly to His troubled disciples. He said, "Do not let your heart be troubled; believe in God, believe also in Me. In My Father's house are many dwelling places; if it were not so, I would have told you; for I go to prepare a place for you. If I go and prepare a place for you, I will come again and receive you to Myself, that where I am, there you may be also."

The Lord Jesus will one day come back to the earth and set up His kingdom forever. This is the culmination of God's certain plan. As believers, we have read the last chapter of the book and know how everything will come out.

Guess what? God *wins*. And those of us who are trusting in Him win too. It's a magnificent ending followed by an incomprehensible new beginning.

But what about all of the terrible things that will take place between now and the earthly return of the Lord? What shall we do about these things as we move closer and closer to difficult times?

This is where we take our cues from the prophet Jeremiah. God gave Jeremiah the job of declaring His judgment upon the nation of Judah. Right from the get-go, both God and Jeremiah knew the people weren't going to like the message—or the messenger. Hard times were on their way. It had to sicken Jeremiah as it would sicken Daniel. So what was he supposed to do?

Run?

Take early retirement?

Move to New Zealand?

God told him exactly what He wanted him to do in Jeremiah 1:17: "But you, dress yourself for work; arise, and say to them everything that I command you. Do not be dismayed by them, lest I dismay you before them."

In a day of rapidly approaching hard times, God told Jeremiah to get up, get dressed, and go to work. And we are to do the same. We are not to sit around, paralyzed with fear. We are not to waste our time by letting our imaginations run riot over what might happen to us or our children as America moves further and further away from biblical Christianity. And we are not to spend our time doing detailed studies trying to figure out the identity of the Antichrist. What a waste of precious time and energy!

So what are we to do? Simply stay faithful at our assigned posts. We're to keep showing up, working hard, and trusting in the promises and timing of a God who loves us. We need to stay the course, control our thoughts and imaginations, think biblically, and realize that a good and wise God is working out His good and wise plan. And in the midst of that plan, He will provide exactly what we need at the moment we need it. In other words, we must discipline our minds to focus on what is certain and in concrete:

His providence is certain.

His promises are certain.

And His plan is certain.

Once again, this is why Jesus told us not to worry about our lives. Our Father has us covered.

"But wait a minute!" you may be saying to yourself. "I've been laid off, and I don't have a clue how I'll find another job. I've lost over 40 percent of my retirement savings. My business is barely making it—and I'm the only guy in America who isn't getting a bailout. *What do you mean, don't worry about my life?* I've already taken a huge financial hit. I *have* to worry about my life! How in the world am I going to make it? I can't keep taking these financial losses!"

If that's where your thoughts have been in recent days, I'd like to ask you to take a break from the anxiety and go for a little walk with an old friend of mine.

A Lesson from George Müller

One of my favorite books is *The Autobiography of George Müller*. The sub-title of the book is "A Million and a Half in Answer to Prayer." Müller established an orphanage in England that took care of 120,000 orphans over a period of sixty-three years. The amazing thing about Müller was that he genuinely believed in the providence of God, the promises of God, and the plan of God.

He wanted people to know that God is the *living God* and that He can be trusted to fulfill His promises. So at the onset of starting his orphanage, Müller determined that he would never ask for money to support his work. Instead, he would simply go to his Father in prayer and tell Him about the needs.

Müller kept a meticulous diary that recorded the needs of the orphanage and the daily balances in the account. He trusted in God alone to meet the financial needs of the orphans, and then he kept careful track of the exact details of God's provisions and answers. As a result, he taught many believers all over the world that they, too, could trust the living God to meet their needs.

On one occasion Müller received a letter from a couple who had sustained a significant financial loss. The vast majority of their assets and cash was gone. They asked Müller for his wisdom on how they should respond to this great burden, which had really set them back on their heels financially.

Müller provided a very unusual diagnosis of their situation. But his "cure" was even more astonishing than his diagnosis. Müller commented that ...

> a heavy [financial] loss should lead us to pause and ponder,
> and consider what the Lord's voice to us is in it. Perhaps the

reason is, that we lived too much as owners and possessors, instead of stewards for the Lord, and that, therefore, He was obliged to take part of that, which we possess, from us. If so, let us be benefited by the loss. But suppose this is not the reason; suppose the Lord allowed the loss only to take place for the trial of our faith and patience, yet we should (while meekly bowing, under the hand of God) say to ourselves that the Lord might have taken all, instead of part, and that, therefore, we ought to make good use of our stewardship respecting the means which are still left to us.[8]

What, then, should this couple do as a result of their loss? How should they respond? George Müller answered that if it were he, he would give a thanks offering to the Lord because the Lord had not taken everything. God was very gracious in that He had only taken a part of their finances when He could have taken everything.

They considered his counsel and then decided to give a thanks offering to the Lord of one hundred pounds—not a small gift at all! Müller then commented on his advice to the couple and the outcome of their decision to give a generous thanks offering:

Well, dear reader, what do you think of this? You think, perhaps, this was very strange. Yes, it was strange, according to the principles of this world; but what will you think when I tell you, that these Christian friends have had that one hundred pounds repaid not merely tenfold, twentyfold, not a hundredfold, but far more than a thousandfold![9]

In these days of an economic meltdown—days that try men's souls— that is a testimony of God's provision that actually lifts your soul. That couple experienced the favor of God nearly 150 years ago, yet that story of God's providence and His promises still brings encouragement to families today. And consider this: What happened through that loss, the sacrificial gift, and the bounty that returned to them as a result were all part of God's plan in the life of this couple.

Did they sustain a major financial loss? Yes.

Do you think they worried about their economic future when they incurred the loss? Of course they did.

Did they follow the advice of a wise Christian man who knew the Lord's faithfulness firsthand? Yes, they did.

In giving a significant thanks offering in the midst of a major loss, did they trust the providence and promises of God? Absolutely.

Did they know what the outcome was going to be? Of course they didn't.

Did they have a clue that you would be reading their story today and finding encouragement for you to trust God in your own financial uncertainty? No, they had no clue you would be reading this 150 years later.

But God did—and it was part of His certain plan.

Are these the times that try men's souls? Absolutely. Is it possible to see the living God still work in a way that will thrill your soul? You know that it is.

I would not be surprised if this husband and wife had, throughout the years of their marriage, prayed and asked God to use them. They were people who obviously loved the Lord and were quick to obey godly counsel. And people like that tend to be people who have a deep-seated desire to be used by God.

That's just what happened. That couple *was* used by God; their story has given you hope that God will be faithful to you even as He was faithful to them. In the last several minutes, your anxiety level has dramatically decreased, hasn't it?

So the Lord definitely used that man and his wife even today in your own life. Their prayer to be used was answered. But it was part of God's plan that this would all begin with a major financial loss in their lives.

It was a brutally difficult time that tried their souls.

But God was simply setting something up in order to thrill their souls.

If He did it for them as they faced their giant uncertainty, why wouldn't He do it for you?

Chapter Two

Giants

"God gets His best soldiers out of the highlands of affliction."
—*C. H. Spurgeon*

If you want to be used—really picked up and significantly utilized—by the living God, you're going to have to fight the giants.

If you think that sounds simplistic, you're right.

It is simple. But it's also the truth.

Joshua and Caleb were *used* by God. They didn't squander or waste their lives. They were used, made a difference, contributed, gave more than they took, and, consequently, their lives are remembered and valued to this day. Why?

Because they were willing to fight the giants.

You probably know the story. Joshua and Caleb were part of a twelve-man team sent out by Moses to do some advance reconnaissance work in the land of Canaan. The children of Israel had just left hundreds of years of slavery in Egypt and were headed to the Promised Land, the land of Canaan. In Numbers 13, God told Moses to pick a leader from each of the twelve tribes in order to do special ops in the land.

The twelve men completed the mission and returned to give their report to Moses and the people of Israel. They reported that it was a fabulous land of milk and honey. They even brought a cluster of grapes out with them—a cluster so heavy it took two men to carry it. But then they got down to the nitty-gritty:

> However, the people who dwell in the land are strong, and the cities are fortified and very large. And besides, we saw the descendants of Anak there. The Amalekites dwell in the land of the Negeb. The Hittites, the Jebusites, and the Amorites dwell in the hill country. And the Canaanites dwell by the sea, and along the Jordan.
>
> But Caleb quieted the people before Moses and said, "Let us go up at once and occupy it, for we are well able to overcome it." Then the men who had gone up with him said, "We are not able to go up against the people, for they are stronger than we are." (vv. 28–31)

These ten spies are quaking in their boots. All of these different tribes of -ites have given them the heebie-jeebies. The battle hasn't even begun, and these guys are already looking for the locker room.

But they weren't done yet with their cowardly report. The old King James Version does the best job of capturing the trembling in their hearts and the shaking of their voices:

> But the men that went up with him said, "We be not able to go up against the people; for they are stronger than we."
>
> And they brought up an evil report of the land which they had searched unto the children of Israel, saying, "The land, through which we have gone to search it, is a land that eateth up the inhabitants thereof; and all the people that we saw in it are men of a great stature.

"And there we saw the giants, the sons of Anak, which come of the giants: and we were in our own sight as grasshoppers, and so we were in their sight." (vv. 31–33)

Did these ten men go on to be used by God?

Did they ever inspire anyone by their example?

Did they ever lead men into battle?

Were they remembered as men of honor and courage?

Are you kidding me?

Notables

Out of all the two million men, women, and children in Israel, just twelve men were chosen to go on the mission. To be selected was a notable honor. To be notable is "to be significant enough to deserve attention or to be recorded."

These twelve men had the attention of the nation. Undoubtedly, all the hopes and fears, dreams and desires of the nation rested on them and their response to what they had encountered in God's land of promise. So they were at least "notable" enough to be selected for the job and to be recorded in the pages of Old Testament history.

To be selected as one of the twelve was a notable achievement and honor. As it happens, however, the only reason these guys were notable was because they insisted they were "not able."[1]

You may have already observed that *notable* and *not able* are spelled exactly the same way. The only difference is an extra space between the *t* and the *a*.

Notable ... not able.

These men not only convinced themselves they were "not able" to follow God's plan, but they also convinced the whole nation, by throwing them into a panic.

Panicked leadership is stupid leadership. It's sort of like saying we need a $750 billion bailout and we need it tomorrow—or the entire nation will collapse economically.

These ten men are some of the most celebrated losers in the entire Bible. And it was all because they refused to fight the giants. They clung to the lie that they were "not able."

Yes, there were giants in the land. That was a fact that even Joshua and Caleb verified. These -ites were bigger, meaner, nastier, and more intimidating than probably any other race of people on the face of the earth. They were notoriously cruel and wicked, and they would show no mercy in combat. What's more, they were huge.

I live in Texas, and a lot of guys down here drink beer in longneck bottles. These sons of Anak were so tall that they were literally known as "long necked." The ten spies described them as giants, or literally "men of many measures."[2] In other words, it took a lot of inches to measure these monsters.

And this was no one-man freak show. There was an entire tribe—a large clan of Neanderthal semi-mastodons that would crush Israel before they knew what hit them. Or … so the ten spies reported.

Make no mistake. The Anakim were legitimate giants, with size 25 sandals to prove it. And they so intimidated the ten spies, who began to see themselves not as men, but as grasshoppers.

Modern-Day Giants

Every man who desires to be used by God will face the giants.

Do you desire to be used by God? It's what gives meaning to a man's life.

Well then, if that's what you desire, you can count on this fact with absolute certainty: You *are* going to fight the giants. There's just no way around it. Just ask Joshua and Caleb—or Samuel Adams and John Hancock. But when it comes to fighting giants, nobody knew more about that than King David and his mighty men.

David faced the Philistine giant Goliath and zipped a line drive straight into his forehead. Then David took Goliath's own sword and cut off his head. That was the end of Goliath and the start of David's ascent. And there's no question that David was used by God. But first he had to fight the giant.

Years later, David faced another oversized Philistine. This new giant, with the endearing name of Ishbi-benob, came straight at David on the battlefield. Before David even had a chance to respond, Abishai stepped in and brought down the monster himself. It was at this point that David's men realized how valuable he was and that he would always be a target for the Philistines. They urged him to take a step back from the battlefield and, from that point forward, to let them take on the giants. And that's just what happened.[3]

To his credit, Abishai was willing to fight the giant, and God used him to save David's life.[4] But it wasn't over yet. There were three more Philistine giants who decided to come after David and Israel.

The next one was an ugly cuss by the name of Saph, and this time another one of David's soldiers by the name of Sibbecai stepped up and took out this incredible hulk.[5]

Sibbecai was willing to fight the giant. He, too, was used by God.

No sooner had Sibbecai taken down Saph, than the Philistines sent in the next monster. This guy was the brother of Goliath, and he was looking to avenge the death of his big brother (no pun intended). Elhanan, another soldier in David's band, killed him.[6]

Elhanan was willing to fight the giants. And like the others, God used Elhanan in a strategic way.

Here it is again: If you have a desire in your heart to be picked up and used by the living God in your life, you can't expect to stroll through the sunshine and daisies for the rest of your years. If you really want a life of usefulness to God, you have to be ready to fight. You must be willing to take on the giants that come lumbering into your path to block your way and stop your progress.

David had a nephew by the name of Jonathan, no doubt named after David's best friend, and when the Philistines sent the next giant in off the bench to threaten David (where did all of these guys come from?), it was Jonathan who stepped up. We don't know the name of this Philistine giant, but we're told he had six fingers on each hand and six toes on each foot. I guess they could have nicknamed him "24." He was the latest, greatest Philistine giant, and like the others, he, too, went down (2 Sam. 21:20–21).

Jonathan was willing to fight the giant. Therefore, we find yet one more guy who was used by God. He stepped in and put his life on the line.

These four mighty men aren't widely known today. Even in their own nation, they weren't awarded with plaques and bronze busts put up in the Pro Giant-Fighters Hall of Fame. Nevertheless, they did become legends in their own time because God used them. And it was all due to the fact that they were willing to fight the giants.

Natural Giant Reflux

There are two normal, natural, and instinctive responses to a threatening giant.

The first is *intimidation.*

The second is *inadequacy.*

The first hint that the ten spies were intimidated pops right out of their own words in Numbers 13:31 (NASB): "We are not able to go up against the people, for they are too strong for us."

The moment they said "we are not able," they were toast. And why were they not able? Well, to their way of thinking, it was pretty simple: The people "are too strong for us."

When I was in seventh grade, my family moved to a new town, and I enrolled in a new school. And that's when I encountered my first giant. His name was Harold, and he was long necked. I never measured him, but he was somewhere between 6'1" and 6'3". We were both twelve years old, but I was somewhere around 5'6" at the time. And he outweighed me by a good forty pounds.

Harold was big, he was mean, and he had twelve fingers and twelve toes. (Or so it seemed.) Almost immediately after laying eyes on me, he decided that his big mission in life was to make young Steve Farrar's life miserable to the max. He began to badger me and pick on me. Now if he had been within a few inches of me, I probably would have had a different response. But this guy was not only big and ugly—he was also mean. I knew there was absolutely no way in the world I could take this guy. I was *not able* to handle him. He was too strong for me.

So yes, I got intimidated.

And then I became paralyzed, because I was acutely aware of my own inadequacies. Now I was a fair athlete, and in my previous school, nobody messed with me. But when I compared myself to this guy, I became like a grasshopper. We were only twelve, but this guy was shaving twice a day. And the more I looked at him, the smaller I became. I was frozen by my own inadequacies.

And because I was so focused on my own inadequacies, I began to view myself as a grasshopper. Not long after that, Harold began to view me as a grasshopper. And then, so did the other guys. There was a ripple effect going on here that was getting me in deeper and deeper.

In my gut, I wanted to move back to my hometown. I wanted to go back to my other school. I wanted to flee. But there was no going back.

Eventually, I was going to have to fight the giant.

And so I did.

With one—and only one—providential punch, Harold went down. And he not only went down, but he never bothered me again. I was more shocked than he was.

The Giants of Life

David had to fight more than one giant in his life—and so will you. But the giants that we take on won't have six fingers on each hand and six toes on each foot.

We fight twenty-first–century giants, a diverse tribe of leering, mocking adversaries that threaten our peace, well-being, and very existence.

- There are giant diseases.
- There are giant disappointments.
- There are giant depressions.
- There are giant addictions.
- There are giant financial reversals.
- There are giant career setbacks.
- There are giant family breakdowns.
- There are giant personal failures.

The man who is used by God will not be free from pain and suffering—not by a long shot. In fact, some of that pain and suffering will be of his own making. And when you are facing a giant that is of your own making, well, that is the bitterest fight you will ever wage.

The man who desires to be used by God will face not one giant in his life, but many. That's the nature of the Christian life. It's a journey from faith to faith, or to put it another way, from giant to giant.

The Greatest Giant

Heart attack, loss of job, a wife with cancer, a son in jail, fighting off a foreclosure—those are all legitimate giants. But what is the greatest giant of all? I teach a men's study in Dallas on Wednesday evenings, and I recently asked that question of the men: "What is the greatest giant of them all?"

When I asked for verbal feedback, it came fast and furious. The answers ricocheted from every corner of the room.

Pride!

Pornography!

Lust!

Guilt!

Regret!

Failure!

Betrayal!

I interrupted the responses and said, "Those are very good answers—very wise answers—but they are all wrong. What else have you got? What is the greatest giant of them all?"

Selfish ambition!

Greed!

The love of money!

Multiple divorces!

Growing up without a father!

An ex-wife who degrades you before the children!

Failing as a father!

Lying!

Breaking a trust!

Fear!

I broke in and said, "I want to commend you for those answers. They aren't superficial, and they are gut-level honest. And those are all big giants. But once again they're all wrong. Let me give you the answer. *The biggest giant of them all is God.*"

And just that quickly, the room of several hundred men grew very quiet. In fact, you could have heard a pin drop as the reality of the answer penetrated the mind of every man in the room.

Every man has fought and is fighting giants. And make no mistake, these giants are *huge*. Sometimes, however, in the process of grappling with these intimidating, overwhelming giants, we forget the greatest Giant.

God is the greatest of all the giants.

Joshua and Caleb knew that, and that's why they stood up and spoke against the panic of the other ten spies.

Samuel Adams and John Hancock knew it as well, and that's why they stood and spoke against tyranny in the name of almighty God.

God is the trump card of your life. It doesn't matter what giant you may be facing—booze, porn, guilt, lying, cocaine, failure, invading armies, whatever—God trumps your giant. He will always trump the giants—every single one of them. But we can so quickly forget that He is there.

After the recent presidential election, some Christians were elated and some were depressed. Many who were depressed expressed great concern over the continuing survival of our democracy. Now that's a major giant.

Samuel Adams and John Hancock wanted a democratic nation to be born. I don't know of any serious Christian who doesn't want it to survive.

So how do you defeat this particular giant? You go to Daniel 2:20–21:

> Daniel answered and said: "Blessed be the name of God forever and ever, to whom belong wisdom and might. He changes times and seasons; he removes kings and sets up kings."

Three Questions

There are three questions that must be answered from this text. Without employing any hype or oversell here, I can tell you that the answers to these three questions bring staggering perspective and legitimate peace to those who are troubled by the outcome of any election.

Question 1: How much wisdom does God have?

The answer is that He has *all* wisdom. Not some wisdom and not most wisdom. He has all wisdom. God never loses His wisdom, never makes a poor decision, and has never (and I say this with all reverence) put His head in His hands and said to Himself, "How could I have been so stupid?" God has never done that and never will. But we do it all the time.

Frank Zappa, a sixties rock musician, once observed, "Some scientists claim that hydrogen, because it is so plentiful, is the basic building block of the universe. I dispute that. I say there is more stupidity than hydrogen, and that is the basic building block of the universe."[7]

God isn't like us. He has never made a mistake. He has no blind spots. He doesn't need counseling.

He *is* wisdom.

Now let's get back to the election. Half of the country was deliriously happy and half the country was clinically depressed. If you found yourself in the latter group, may I put the question to you again: How much wisdom does God have? Daniel declares He has it *all.*

So if God has all wisdom, then why would you be depressed? May I suggest to you that one of the main reasons is that we don't know our Bibles? Please pay very close attention to the wise counsel of J. I. Packer:

> Wisdom is divinely wrought in those, and those only, who apply themselves to God's revelation. "Thou through thy commandments hast made me wiser than my enemies" declares the psalmist, "I have more understanding than all my teachers." Why?—"for thy testimonies are my meditation" (Psalm 119:99f). So Paul admonishes the Colossians: "Let the word of Christ dwell in you richly in all wisdom" (Colossians 3:16). How are we men of the twentieth century to do this? By soaking ourselves in the Scriptures….
>
> It is to be feared that many today that profess to be Christ's never learn wisdom, through failure to attend sufficiently to God's written word…. William Gouge, the Puritan, read fifteen chapters regularly each day. The late Archbishop T. C. Hammond used to read right through the Bible once a quarter. How long is it since you read right through the Bible? Do you spend as much time with the Bible each day as you do even with the newspaper? What fools some of us are!—and we remain fools all of our lives, simply because we will not take the trouble to do what has to be done to receive the wisdom which is God's free gift.[8]

We lose our wisdom when we forget that God has all wisdom. And we lose the handle on that very important piece of information when we forget our Bibles.

Question 2: How much power does God have?

Quite a bit of power? Most power? Almost all power? No, you know those answers don't even come close. Daniel 2:20 declares that He has all—*all*—power.

So let me get this straight. He's got all wisdom, and He's got all power. That's quite a combination. That's quite a God. In fact, that's what you call a great God. He's wise, and He's omnipotent. That's why He's the trump card over every giant.

Omnipotence is a big word that can save your life. It's the CPR of the Christian life. I'm not kidding—that one word can save you when a giant is threatening to stomp on your windpipe. I'll let my friend Wayne Grudem explain:

> God's omnipotence means that God is able to do all his holy will. The word omnipotence is derived from two Latin words, *omni*, "all," and *potens*, "powerful" and means "all-powerful." Omnipotence has reference to his own power to do what he decides to do.
>
> This power is frequently mentioned in Scripture. God is "The LORD, strong and mighty, the LORD, mighty in battle!" (Psalm 24:8). The rhetorical question "Is anything too hard for the LORD?" (Genesis 18:14; Jeremiah 32:27) certainly implies (in the contexts in which it occurs) that nothing is too hard for the Lord. In fact, Jeremiah says to God, "Nothing is too hard for you" (Jeremiah 32:17).

Paul says that God is "able to do far more abundantly beyond all that we ask or think" (Ephesians 3:20), and God is called the Almighty (2 Corinthians 6:18; Revelation 1:8), a term (Greek: *pantokrator*) that suggests the possession of all power and authority. Furthermore, the angel Gabriel says to Mary, "With God nothing will be impossible" (Luke 1:37), and Jesus says, "With God all things are possible" (Matthew 19:26).[9]

Do you know the song "How Great Is Our God"? From time to time, I catch myself singing that song as I'm driving around in my truck. That song does a tremendous job of reminding us of His greatness. The ten spies were stupid because they didn't think about His greatness and the greatness of His name. When you stop to consider the situation, these men had no excuse. Hadn't they just witnessed the ten mighty plagues God sent on the Egyptian nation, persuading a hard-hearted pharaoh to release all the Hebrew slaves? And hadn't they just seen God split the Red Sea, allowing the whole nation to cross on dry ground—and then allowing those mighty water walls to collapse, drowning the pursuing Egyptian army? They weren't just stupid, they had very, very short memories.

Our God is the Lord God Almighty. He has all power and all authority. So when the question is asked, "Is anything too hard for the Lord?" it doesn't need an answer. If He has all power and all authority, then obviously, nothing, absolutely nothing, is too hard for Him.

Does that mean, then, that God can do anything? No, it doesn't mean that. That's kind of a curveball, isn't it? I'll let Grudem explain:

There are some things that God cannot do. God cannot will or do anything that would deny his own character. That is why the definition of omnipotence is stated in

terms of God's ability to do "all his holy will." It is not
absolutely everything that God is able to do, but everything that is consistent with his character. For example,
God cannot lie. In Titus 1:2, he is called (literally) "the
unlying God" or the "God who never lies." The author
of Hebrews says that in God's oath and promise "it is
impossible for God to lie" (Hebrews 6:18, author's translation). Second Timothy 2:13 says of Christ, "He cannot
deny himself." Furthermore, James says "God cannot be
tempted with evil and he himself tempts no one" (James
1:13). Thus, God cannot lie, sin, deny himself, or be
tempted with evil. He cannot cease to exist, or cease
to be God, or act in a way inconsistent with any of his
attributes.[10]

So God can't do anything—anything that's wrong, that is. He will never
deceive you or promise to do something and then let you down. Those are
things He cannot do. And He cannot cease to exist; He will always be, and
He will always be there for you. Now that's a great God.

So what about the giants? It's kind of laughable to even bring them up,
isn't it? Nothing is too hard for the Lord. So do you see why it's so incredibly stupid to say that God is "not able"?

Joshua and Caleb lived many hundreds of years prior to Daniel. Yet
the truths about God that Daniel declared in 2:20–21 were the same truths
that anchored the faith of Joshua and Caleb. And this is why those huge,
fearsome warriors of Canaan didn't intimidate them. These two men knew
their God. They knew He had all wisdom and all power. When the ten
gave their report to Moses and the congregation, fear swept through the
congregation of Israel like a firestorm. The people became absolutely and
utterly panicked.

Now, watch the leadership of Joshua and Caleb. As we will see, these two men would be greatly used by God throughout their lives. They are models to us of what a man who is used by God looks like.

When the panic rose as the spies gave their terrifying report, Caleb beat Joshua to the punch and spoke up first. The Bible says, "But Caleb quieted the people before Moses and said, 'Let us go up at once and occupy it, for we are well able to overcome it'" (Num. 13:30).

The ten said, "We are not able."

Caleb took strong exception to that summary. Standing up against the ten faithless spies and the panicked masses, he shouted, "Wait a minute! We *are* able! Of course we are! These guys are idiots, and they're talking utter nonsense!" (Farrar loose translation.)

All the spies did agree on one thing: The giants were real. They had seen them. So there was no disputing the enormity and strength of this enemy. The nub of this issue was their *response* to the giants.

Joshua and Caleb responded with *sense*.

The ten responded with *stupidity*.

You've heard of the Jane Austen book *Sense and Sensibility* (if you haven't, I guarantee you that your wife has). Well, this report from the twelve Israelites wasn't sense and sensibility; it was *sense and stupidity*.

Joshua and Caleb had sense—the other ten guys were flat-out stupid. They either didn't think that God trumped every other giant, or they didn't think at all. They just panicked. And when the ten leaders panicked, the people fell like a line of dominoes, and *everyone* panicked (Num. 14:1–4).

> Then all the congregation raised a loud cry, and the people
> wept that night. And all the people of Israel grumbled
> against Moses and Aaron. The whole congregation said
> to them, "Would that we had died in the land of Egypt!
> Or would that we had died in this wilderness! Why is the

LORD bringing us into this land, to fall by the sword? Our
wives and our little ones will become a prey. Would it not
be better for us to go back to Egypt?" And they said to one
another, "Let us choose a leader and go back to Egypt."

This hysterical, unnerving report from the ten spies not only led to
a mass panic on the part of the people, but it also led to mass stupidity. Remember Jim Jones and Jonestown? These people were all lining up
to drink the poisoned Kool-Aid. Let's briefly break down their thought
process:

It would have been better if we had died in Egypt? That doesn't make a lot
of sense. Return to slavery? How could that possibly have been better?

Well, we should have died in the wilderness! Are you sure about that?

Why is God bringing us to this land to die by the sword? Is that what God
is doing? Didn't He say He was going to give you houses you didn't build
and crops you didn't plant? What makes you think He's going to let you
die by the sword?

*Our wives and kids are going to go through terrible suffering—we should
choose a leader and go back to Egypt. Let's get everyone registered to vote and
then they can all vote early and often. And then we can elect the leader we want
to take us all back to Egypt so Pharaoh can make us slaves again.*

This isn't just panic—it is insanity. (And when you think about it, panic
and insanity are separated by only the thinnest of lines.)

Now watch how Joshua and Caleb stepped in and tried to stop the
panic in verses 5–9. Attempting to reason with a mob that was almost ready
to spin out of control, the two faithful spies began to remind the people of
the facts about their situation.

Then Moses and Aaron fell on their faces before all the
assembly of the congregation of the people of Israel. And

Joshua the son of Nun and Caleb the son of Jephunneh, who were among those who had spied out the land, tore their clothes and said to all the congregation of the people of Israel, "The land, which we passed through to spy it out, is an exceedingly good land. If the LORD delights in us, he will bring us into this land and give it to us, a land that flows with milk and honey. Only do not rebel against the LORD. And do not fear the people of the land, for they are bread for us. Their protection is removed from them, and the LORD is with us; do not fear them."

Joshua and Caleb have one focus and it is *God*.

They reminded the people of what God had said and what God would do.

But the people weren't really thinking at this point; they were simply letting their anxiety get further and further out of control. The truth is, they *wanted* to be swept along in their panic and they didn't want to think. They didn't want to listen to truth, and they resented anyone who tried to reason with them. So what does the mob of hundreds of thousands of panicked people do in response to Joshua and Caleb?

"Then all the congregation said to stone them with stones" (v. 10).

When facing down a giant—any giant—your first and most important response is to *think*. Christianity is about facts. You don't throw away your mind—you kick it into gear. This is where what you believe about God is extremely important. He claims to have all power, but if He doesn't, it's your funeral. He claims to be in absolute control, but if He's not, then He can't protect you and give you victory.

On the other hand, if He *does* have power, and if He truly is in control of everything … well, that changes everything, doesn't it?

I'll come back to my main point: If you're going to be used by God, you're going to have to fight the giants. But in order to fight the giants, you first have to "be strong in the Lord and in the strength of his might."[11] If you aren't strong in the Lord, you may as well plan your own memorial service, because you won't stand a chance against any kind of giant. The ten weren't strong in the Lord—and that's why they said, "We're not able." But contrast those ten losers with Joshua and Caleb, who were strong in the Lord.

Hear the wise words of Dr. Martyn Lloyd-Jones:

> There is no better way of giving a proof of the truth of the Gospel than that we should "be strong in the Lord and in the power of His might," than that we should triumph and prevail.
>
> To live aright is difficult, and when we see someone who is succeeding, someone who can stand against the enticements and insinuations of evil, someone who is not carried away off his feet by the popular thing, someone who remains steadfastly for truth and for everything that is worthy, we are greatly encouraged. It undoubtedly has a great effect on those who are looking on.[12]

This is why we are considering the example of Joshua and Caleb three thousand years later!

This is what Ephesians 6:10–11 (NASB) means when it says to "be strong in the Lord and in the strength of His might. Put on the full armor of God, so that you will be able to stand firm against the schemes of the devil."

And then Paul immediately spoke of the various pieces of armor that we are to put on as we enter into spiritual battle. But there is something critical that cannot be missed. You can put on the helmet of salvation, the belt of truth, the breastplate of righteousness, the shield of faith, and strap on the cleated boots of salvation—but if you aren't first "strong in the Lord," you're going down. You will be defeated, and the giants will use you for a football.

What does it mean to be "strong in the Lord and in the strength of His might"? It means that in your mind and in your heart you know that *He is omnipotent.* You know—you have it locked in your mind, cemented in your soul—that He has all power and all authority. You know that nothing or no one in this universe—or whatever universe there may be—can stand against Him. In other words, to be strong in the Lord is to know and *think* about His strength, His power, and His character. That's the place to start. You have to *think!*

When you *think* about who God is and the fact that He has all wisdom and all power and that He is the Giant that trumps every other giant, you are doing something very important: You are applying your faith.

Joshua and Caleb weren't stupid, they weren't nearsighted, and they weren't in denial. They knew perfectly well that the giants were out there; they had seen them with their own eyes. *But they also knew their God was the Lord God Almighty.* They had seen His power at work when He delivered them out of Egypt. They saw His awesome power as He sent the ten plagues and then opened the Red Sea. And they remembered how He kept Pharaoh's special forces off them while they crossed by settling in a heavy darkness over them (Josh. 24:7). He delivered them by the power of His mighty hand.

They remembered His might and used their minds to think about His awesome power. Holding these truths in their thoughts, they knew—beyond any faintest shadow of doubt—that the Lord God Almighty would unleash His great power for them against those Canaanite armored goons. That's why they knew they were well able to defeat the giants.

How about you? Do you really believe that? If you do, then like Joshua and Caleb, you will see God do great things on your behalf.

Question 3: Who determines the outcome of every election?

Allow me to give you a hint. It's not Gallup or Zogby, it's not how many dead people voted in Chicago or how many hanging chads are counted in Dade County, Florida. It's not who spent the most money, who is the most savvy with the Internet, or who had the best attack ads.

The One who determines the outcome of every election is God. Let's go back to Daniel 2:20–21: "Daniel answered and said: 'Blessed be the name of God forever and ever, to whom belong wisdom and might. He changes times and seasons; he removes kings and sets up kings.'"

God changes the times and the seasons. That's why I believe that global warming will not destroy this planet. God promised that wouldn't happen in Genesis 8:21–22:

> And when the LORD smelled the pleasing aroma, the LORD said in his heart, "I will never again curse the ground because of man, for the intention of man's heart is evil from his youth. Neither will I ever again strike down every living creature as I have done. While the earth remains, seedtime and harvest, cold and heat, summer and winter, day and night, shall not cease."

Here's a little news bulletin for radical environmentalists: The earth will remain until God accomplishes His plan for the ages. And until then, the seasons and the cycles of life will obey Him. "Seedtime and harvest, cold and heat, summer and winter, day and night, shall not cease." The heat won't overcome the cold, and the cold won't overcome the heat. He has ordained the course the seasons will run and the future of the earth.

And that includes every king, emperor, president, prime minister, and tin-pot, banana-republic dictator.

God removes kings and sets them up. He, and He alone, determines the outcome of presidential elections.

Yes, I still voted. But I did so knowing that His will would be done. And not only did He determine the outcome of the election, but He will also determine the actions of the one who sits in the Oval Office.

> The king's heart is like channels of water in the hand of
> the LORD;
>> He turns it wherever He wishes. (Prov. 21:1 NASB)

God is working His plan for the world, the nations, and your life. That's why Job said, "He performs what is appointed for me."[13] And that sovereign detailed plan is also described in the words of Ephesians 1:11: "In him we have obtained an inheritance, having been predestined according to the purpose of him *who works all things* according to the counsel of his will." Did you see those italics that I placed in that verse? I did that so you wouldn't miss that God's plan is exhaustive.

John J. Murray comments briefly and biblically on God's plan:

> The plan is perfect. Everything that God does is perfect. It may not appear to me at times to be perfect but it is, because it will ultimately lead to the greater glory of God.
>
> The plan is exhaustive. It includes everything. It is worked out in a situation where everything is under the control of God. It extends to the smallest and most casual things. "The very hairs of your head are all numbered" (Matthew 10:30).
>
> The plan is for my ultimate good. Everyone who loves God has the assurance that "all things work together for

good" (Romans 8:28). If God is for me, who can be against me? The opposition does not count. The gracious purpose of God will certainly be accomplished in my life.

The plan is secret. God alone knows what is going to happen in advance because He purposed it all. Every detail was fixed before I was born. God hides it from me until it happens. I discover it day by day as the plan unfolds. This is the unfolding of His secret will for my life.[14]

Are the giants we face part of God's plan? Absolutely. No giant has ever taken our God by surprise … so we don't need to fear.

Our Father and God is the Giant of giants.

He is the Great Notable who makes us able.

Case closed.

Chapter Three

Gravitas

"Courage is being scared to death—and saddling up anyway."
—*John Wayne*

inesh D'Souza tells the story of the spoiled wife whose husband was a wealthy London aristocrat. When she was first told of Darwin's claim that man had descended from an apelike creature, she remarked, "My dear, let us hope that it is not true, but if it is, let us pray that it may not become widely known."[1]

J. Robert Oppenheimer had something hidden in his past life that he prayed would not become widely known. You may remember Oppenheimer as the man who became known as "the father of the atomic bomb." Selected in 1942 to be the scientific director of the Manhattan Project, it was his task to bring together more than three thousand scientists and engineers for the purpose of developing the atomic bomb. And that's just what he did. Celebrated as one of the preeminent scientists of the twentieth century, this brilliant man was placed in charge of one of the most sensitive and dangerous projects ever undertaken in all of history.

His qualifications and biography are impressive. I have before me his biography, which can be found at atomicarchive.com. Allow me to simply give you the first paragraph of the bio—and there's a reason I'm doing so:

Julius Robert Oppenheimer was born in New York City on April 22, 1904. His parents, Julius S. Oppenheimer, a wealthy German textile merchant, and Ella Friedman, an artist, were of Jewish descent but did not observe the religious traditions. He studied at the Ethical Culture Society School, whose physics laboratory has since been named for him, and entered Harvard in 1922, intending to become a chemist, but soon switching to physics. He graduated summa cum laude in 1925 and went to England to conduct research at Cambridge University's Cavendish Laboratory, working under J. J. Thomson.[2]

The biography goes on for five more paragraphs, documenting Oppenheimer's further studies at the University of Gottingen, Harvard, and the California Institute of Technology. He then became an assistant professor at the University of California at Berkeley, where he married Katherine Peuning Harrison, who was a radical student at Berkeley. They were married in 1941. The biography then continues on in much detail about his scholarly research that led to his appointment as director of the Manhattan Project.

So what's the secret that he didn't want to get out? Was it that in 1953 his security clearance was taken away because of his communist sympathies? No, that's not it. You can find that in his biography.

So what was the secret Oppenheimer worked so hard to cover up? Did you catch that one sentence in his bio about him going to England to study at Cambridge University?

While he was a student at Cambridge, he became very frustrated with one of his tutors. The tutor's name was Paul Brackett. He was a brilliant physicist himself and would go on to win the Nobel Prize in 1948. But he was a very demanding teacher, and he kept pushing Oppenheimer in his studies on experimental physics. Oppenheimer hated the subject, and he grew to hate the tutor.

So Oppenheimer took some chemicals from the lab and attempted to poison Paul Brackett. Here was Oppenheimer's secret: *He tried to murder his professor*. The tutor somehow discovered what Oppenheimer had done and did not take the poison. Oppenheimer fully intended to commit premeditated murder. Malcolm Gladwell tells this story in his book *The Outliers*, and as Gladwell puts it, "The university was informed. Oppenheimer was called on the carpet. And what happened next is every bit as unbelievable as the crime itself."[3]

After numerous meetings with Cambridge officials, Oppenheimer convinced them to put him on probation. No charges were filed. He was reprimanded and told to regularly visit a psychiatrist.[4]

Oppenheimer was not only a genius, but he was also incredibly smooth and charming. He was so brilliant that at the age of nine you could ask him a question in Latin, and he would answer you in Greek. And he could project such an attractive and persuasive personality that he could talk his way out of anything—including an attempted-murder charge.

He had it all—brains, intelligence, charm, and persuasiveness. All he was missing was character. A professor is pushing you a little too hard? No problem. You just poison the guy and get him out of the way.

That was the secret that he didn't want to become known. But it certainly came up in the background check when he was being considered by General Leslie Groves to head up the Manhattan Project. Once again, he worked the charm and played the general like a piano. And Groves overlooked his "indiscretion" of attempted murder and put him in charge of the most sensitive project of World War II.

So Oppenheimer's little slip in judgment was no big deal, right? Just a minor character flaw maybe?

As we will see, character is never a minor issue.

In Our Last Episode

In the last chapter, we left Joshua and Caleb facing off with the other
ten spies who, because of their fear and unbelief, had managed to panic
and stampede the entire nation of Israel. I want to go back to this event
described in Numbers 13—14 and ask a question:

What was it that made Joshua and Caleb so different from the other
ten spies? Why did those two stand tall against the giants while the other
guys were looking for their passports? Numbers 13:1 makes it clear that all
twelve of these men were prominent in the nation:

> The LORD spoke to Moses, saying, "Send men to spy out
> the land of Canaan, which I am giving to the people of
> Israel. From each tribe of their fathers you shall send a
> man, every one a chief among them."

Each of the twelve tribes put up their best man, the leaders, the chiefs,
the cream of the crop. These twelve men were the all-stars of Israel. So make
no mistake about it: This reconnaissance team was comprised of gifted, smart,
articulate men who were good with people. These guys pretty much had it all,
and yet ten of them were lacking an essential ingredient: character.

Character was the primary difference between Joshua and Caleb and the
other ten. By their actions the ten revealed themselves to be losers instead of
leaders. They caved under the pressure of the giants. They refused to look at
God and His personal guarantee to deliver them.

These guys flat out didn't have it. They were so inept that they could
have run Fannie Mae or Freddie Mac. In other words, they were useless.
They had no gravitas. There was no weight to their character or substance to
their lives. In their weakness, these men not only trashed their own lives, but
by their actions they also wasted the lives of a whole generation of Israelites.

Everyone from that generation—save Joshua and Caleb—would die in the desert, never setting foot in the land of plenty God had promised them.

I wonder what Winston Churchill would have to say about them?

You might say that Churchill wasn't a man to bear fools gladly; but on the other hand, it wasn't his style to come right out and call someone stupid, either. He would say it in other ways, and do so very creatively.

Of Prime Minister Clement Attlee, Churchill said, "He is a modest man, with much to be modest about." On another occasion, he referred to Attlee as "a sheep in sheep's clothing."

Stanley Baldwin was a prime minister from an earlier era, and of Baldwin he said, "Occasionally he stumbled over the truth but hastily picked himself up as if nothing happened."

Churchill went on to say of Rab Butler, the chancellor of the exchequer, "I am amused by the Chancellor of the Exchequer. He is always patting himself on the back, a kind of exercise that contributes to his excellent physical condition."

Of Prime Minister Arthur Balfour, Churchill observed that "if you wanted nothing done, Arthur Balfour was the best man for the task. There was no equal to him."

And in regard to T. E. Lawrence, who became known as Lawrence of Arabia, Churchill said, "He was not in complete harmony with the normal."[5]

The Character Channel

I'm sure you're aware of the fact that there is a cable channel devoted 24-7 to running cooking shows. The entire channel is devoted to chefs, cooks, recipes, and cooking techniques. That's all there is to it. It's known simply as The Food Channel.

I'd like to see some producer put together the Character Channel. Wouldn't that be great? And I'd give Joshua and Caleb the first prime-time, high-definition slots that became available. God used these men to stand up and give leadership to a situation that had deteriorated into utter chaos. How could they be so confident? How is it that they refused to panic like the others?

These men knew the recipe for godly character, and they had applied it to their lives. That's why Joshua and Caleb were different from the other leaders. Leaders are everywhere; in fact, they're a dime a dozen. But a leader with character is rare indeed.

I think the apostle Paul gives us a glimpse into the character of these two men when he writes to Titus. Now let me be very clear. The passage I'm going to quote never mentions Joshua or Caleb—not by name. But the essential character traits Paul highlights for young Titus in this passage were so obviously resident in the hearts and minds of these two Old Testament leaders. The text is Titus 2:2 (NASB), and it's nothing short of a recipe—a character recipe:

"Older men are to be temperate, dignified, sensible, sound in faith, in love, in perseverance."

Paul puts it out on the table: These are the critical ingredients that must be present in the life of a mature man. This is the man whom God will use. And yes, he does say that he wants these traits to be in the lives of the older men. But that doesn't mean that younger guys are excused from class. It just means that this is the standard you should be shooting for. But it's never too early to begin the process.

Now for the sake of simplicity (and because I've got some preacher in me), I'm going to convert these traits into four words that begin with *s*.

- Sober
- Serious
- Sensible
- Sound—in faith, love, and perseverance

I would submit to you that each of these four traits was present in the lives of Joshua and Caleb. That's why they didn't get stupid when they saw the giants. They were able to keep their heads on straight because they were thinking straight.

Sober

The word translated "temperate" means to be sober. It indicates "a general restraint in indulging desires."[6] Gene Getz is on target when he describes this man as one who (because he restrains his desires) "has a clear perspective on life and a correct spiritual orientation.... Put another way, [the sober or temperate man] does not lose his physical, psychological or physical orientation. He remains stable and steadfast, his thinking is clear. Put in more relevant terms, he is 'calm, cool, and collected' in most situations."[7]

Men who are drunk on alcohol tend not to be "calm, cool, and collected." Guys who drink to excess actually have a great tendency to lose their cool and do things they normally wouldn't.

A lot of men have found that the Lord can not only forgive them for their sins, but also give them the daily power to stay sober (in all aspects of the word). When a man is sober, he is of sound mind, he is thinking straight.

Serious

The text translates this word as "dignified," and the sense here is of a man who is serious about life. Some translations refer to this as "grave." It doesn't mean that a man should be grim about life and never laugh. But it does mean that a man should be serious about his life and his responsibilities to the Lord, his family, and his work. This is a man with gravity in his life; in other words, he's got his feet on the ground. He doesn't live with his head in the clouds. He can be counted on in the clutch.

It reminds me of J. B. Phillips's paraphrase of Ephesians 5:15–17:

> Live life, then, with a due sense of responsibility, not as
> men who do not know the meaning and purpose of life
> but as those who do. Make the best use of your time,
> despite all the difficulties of these days. Don't be vague
> but firmly grasp what you know to be the will of God.

Sensible

This is a sound thinker with his life under control—a man who is neither flippant nor impulsive about life. He lives off certain principles, ordering both his life and his behavior around them.

The word and its different forms, which Paul uses to describe this mark of maturity (*siphon*), are variously translated as sober, sober-minded, of sound mind and judgment, or prudent. One commentator suggests that perhaps the best explanation of what Paul has in mind is found in Romans 12:3: "For through the grace given to me I say to every man among you not to think more highly of himself than he ought to think; but to think so as to have sound judgment (that is, to think soberly, sensibly, or prudently), as God has allotted each man a measure of faith."[8]

The sensible man is a clear thinker who exercises reliable judgment in the daily affairs of life. He's a man who can be looked to in a great crisis. He is mastered by the Master; therefore, he is master of himself. He's not out of control; he's in control under stress and pressure.

Sound in Faith, Love, and Perseverance

To be sound is to be healthy. The sound man is healthy in faith (what he believes), healthy in love (how he treats people), and healthy in perseverance or steadfastness (he's not wandering away from his family or from the truth). You've heard the expression "stay the course"? That's this guy's motto. He won't bail on his commitments or drop his responsibilities.

Now let's try to sum up all of those characteristics. This is a man who has staying power. He is sober and in control of what he puts into his body. He is serious about life, but not so serious that he can't have a good time. He's the kind of man who knows how to have fun, but also knows that there's more to life than seeking fun and pleasure. He has gravitas—he's got his feet firmly planted on the ground. He's not wandering off from his faith or his family. He doesn't chase women. He's a sound thinker with his life under control. He's healthy in what he believes about God, and healthy from his feeding on the Bible. He's healthy with his wife and his kids. If there's a conflict, he moves to repair it. And he is healthy in that he has staying power: When life gets tough, he's not running away or looking for the back door.

Don't you see all of these traits in Joshua and Caleb? I certainly do. This is why they were willing to fight the giants. This is why they didn't panic and run for cover. This is why God used them in such a remarkable way.

Gold Nugget

Just for a moment, let's go back to that expression "sound in faith." This is a phrase that explains the difference between Joshua and Caleb and the ten. Sound in faith, Joshua and Caleb stood against the ten, vainly trying to undo the damage and rally the people to go into the land. Because they were "sound in faith," they were willing to square their shoulders and fight any giant that popped his ugly head up over the horizon. The other guys may have been leaders, but they weren't "sound in faith." So when they saw the giants, every one of them caved.

Faith is believing who God is and what He has said. So who is He? We saw in the last chapter that He is omnipotent—He has all power. But what is this God like? And can He be trusted?

Now watch this: In order to be sound in faith, you have to know who God is and what He is like. In other words, you have to get your facts straight about God's essential character. Joshua and Caleb were in this category. Daniel 11:32 (NASB) demonstrates the difference between Joshua and Caleb and the other ten yo-yos: "The people who know their God will display strength and take action."

John Wycliffe was sound in faith back in the fourteenth century. And he was thoroughly hated for it. Wycliffe was a biblical scholar and pastor who spoke out against the false teaching of the Roman Catholic Church. He declared that the Catholic Church was not the authority, the Bible was. But the common people had no idea what the Bible actually said, because the medieval Catholic Church made sure it was in Latin and only available to church officials.

Wycliffe translated the Bible into the common language, so that it could be read to people throughout England. He actually organized a group of poor Christians, called Lollards, who would go throughout the countryside reading the Bible to villagers and anyone who would listen. The Catholic officials savagely attacked Wycliffe for his work and tried to have him removed from his position at Oxford. In God's providence, however, powerful men stood with him and protected him from every attack.

John Wycliffe died in 1384, but he was so hated that in 1428, his body was exhumed and his bones were burned.[9] They scattered his ashes in the River Swift. But as one writer commented, his ashes were scattered into the Swift, which eventually fed into the sea. And just as his ashes were carried by the sea around the earth, so was the power of his teaching.[10]

How could Wycliffe stand and take on the giant of the Roman Catholic Church? He knew God! In order to display strength and take action in life-threatening situations, one must know God. This describes why Joshua and Caleb stood against the ten and the entire congregation.

They knew God, and they knew what He is like.

Do you?

Let me give you a clue up front: He's not like us. As you read the next few pages, get ready to *think*. You can get this stuff, but it's going to stretch your brain cells a little bit. But you can get it! In fact, it's critical that you do get it; without such knowledge, you won't be sound in faith.

Earlier we looked at the fact that our Lord has all wisdom and all power.

There are four more facts about Him that are equally as important—*if* you're going to be sound in faith.

God Is Self-Existent

Have you ever asked yourself where God came from? The answer to that is that He has always existed. He has all life in Himself, as John 5:26 clearly states: "For as the Father has life in himself, so he has granted the Son also to have life in himself."

But where did He come from?

Incomprehensible as it may be to our finite minds, He didn't "come from" anywhere, because He had no beginning. He has always been, and He will never go out of existence. The self-existence of God "means that God has the ground of existence in Himself, and unlike man, does not depend on anything outside of Himself."[11] In Job 41:11 (NASB), God says, "Who has given to Me that I should repay him? Whatever is under the whole heaven is Mine."

Because He is self-existent, all creatures depend on Him; God, however, depends on no one and nothing. In Psalm 50:10–12 (NASB), God states,

For every beast of the forest is Mine,

    The cattle on a thousand hills.

    I know every bird of the mountains,

    And everything that moves in the field is Mine.

    If I were hungry I would not tell you,

    For the world is Mine, and all it contains.

He owns the oceans and the oil, the mountain goats and the mountains. The entire creation depends upon Him for its existence—but God is dependent on nothing. He is the source of all life and the sustainer of life. Including your life.

God Is Unchanging

This means that "He is forever the same in His divine Being and perfections, and also in His purposes and promises."[12]

In Malachi 3:6, God declares, "For I the LORD do not change."

Sometimes in Scripture we read of God "repenting" of a certain course of action—which naturally seems to us like a change of mind. But as Louis Berkhof stated, "This is only a human way of speaking of God (Exodus 32:14; Jonah 3:10), and really indicates a change in man's relation to God."[13] If that presents a problem for you, ask yourself this question: "Did God *know* that He was going to change His mind before He changed it?" The answer to that question is yes. Therefore, He really didn't change His mind at all; it was always His purpose to do just what He did. It just looks to us (from our finite, human viewpoint) that He changed.

This great God doesn't change in His character or in His promise. Therefore, He can be trusted.

God Is Infinite

"This means that God is not subject to limitations. He is above time.... He is everywhere present, dwells in all His creatures, filling every point of space, but is in no way bound by space."[14]

J. I. Packer specified that "God is limited neither by space (He is everywhere in His fullness continually) nor by time (there is no 'present moment' into which he is locked as we are)." Theologians refer to this as His infinity, His immensity, and His transcendence (1 Kings 8:27; Isa. 40:12–26; 66:1). As He upholds everything in His being, so He has everything everywhere always before His mind, in its own relation to His all-inclusive plan and purpose for every item and every person in His world (Dan. 4:34–35; Eph. 1:11).[15]

This truth is vitally important. Why is it so critical? Because when you are in a crisis and crying out to Him, He will never put you on hold. "He is present everywhere in the fullness of all that He is and all the powers that He has, and needy souls praying to Him anywhere in the world received the same fullness of undivided attention. Because God is omnipresent He is able to share His attention to millions of individuals at the same time."[16]

Are you still there? This stuff is getting a little heavy. You don't have to understand everything here to its fullest extent. But are you getting a sense that God is great and that He is bigger than any giant that could ever come your way? I defy you to name a giant that our great God could not demolish—vaporize—instantaneously. That's why this is so critical. It enables us to *think* and apply our knowledge of God to giants we are facing in life.

Let's take another lap on this stuff.

God Is All Knowing

Proverbs 15:3 (NIV) declares, "The eyes of the LORD are everywhere, keeping watch on the wicked and the good."

God knows "all things possible and actual."[17] In other words, He knows all things that are and all that could be. He is omniscient—"a word that means, 'knowing everything.'"[18]

> He searches all hearts and knows everyone's ways (1 Samuel 16:7; 1 Kings 8:39; 1 Chronicles 28:9; Psalm 139:1–6; Jeremiah 17:10; Luke 16:15; Romans 8:27; Revelation 2:23). In other words, He knows everything about everybody all the time. Also, He knows the future no less than the past and the present, and possible events that never happen no less than the actual events do (1 Samuel 23:9–13; 2 Kings 13:9; Psalm 81:14–15; Isaiah 48:18). Nor does He have to access information about things, as a computer might retrieve a file; all His knowledge is always immediately and directly before His mind. Bible writers stand in awe of the capacity of God's mind in this regard (Psalm 139:1–6; 147:5; Isaiah 40:13–14, 28; cf. Romans 11:33–36).[19]

By the way, if the biblical writers stood in awe of the capacity of God's mind—so should you.

There are many other attributes of God that I have not listed, including His love, His holiness, His truthfulness, His wrath, His wisdom—and on it goes, *forever.*

I have briefly listed just a few attributes in these pages as a means of letting us get a glimpse into God's greatness. We must come to know Him, and the more we know of Him, the more we will worship and honor Him for His infinite greatness and majesty.

Why It Matters

The more you know God, the more you know that He has always existed, that He has all power, that He is everywhere, that He is good, that He never changes, and that He has all wisdom. Now that is a God who can be *trusted*. You see, the more you know who God is, the more sound you will be in faith and truth. And the more sound you are in faith and truth— watch this—the more He will use you! You can be trusted in a crisis not to go off half-cocked like the ten. This is why it is so critical to know Him. When you know Him, you trust Him. And the more you trust Him, the more peace you experience, even in crisis, because you know that He's got your back. Philip Bennett Power was dead-on when he wrote, "God loves trust; it honors Him; he who trusts the most shall sorrow least. If there was continual trust there would be continual peace."[20]

What, then, is the ultimate outcome of knowing God and His attributes? It's Daniel 11:32 (NASB): "The people who know their God will display strength and take action."

When a man displays strength and takes action because he knows God, well, that's a man who is being used by God. And here's the underlying message of that verse: If you want God to *use* you—you must first know who He is. That's the critical element underlying all of this discussion on His attributes.

Sober men, serious men, sensible men, sound men are the men who know God. And because they know Him and think about Him in crisis, they display strength and take action. That takes us right back to Joshua and Caleb. And it's a great place for me to introduce you to Paul Lanier.

Paul Lanier's Giant

Paul Lanier was a friend of mine who fought the giant of Lou Gehrig's disease (ALS) for a year. But even as Paul's body quit on him, he displayed strength and took action. And it was all because Paul threw himself into the Scriptures and a study of God's attributes and His entire Word.

Paul lived off the greatness of God. That's why even when he couldn't move a muscle in his body, God used him. He impacted other men and saw their lives change.

Several months ago, I had the privilege of speaking at Paul Lanier's memorial service. Paul was a medical doctor with a lovely wife and three beautiful daughters. He was also a pilot and loved nothing more than flying with a few friends out to some remote location to hunt for a week at a time. In tremendous physical shape, Paul was a powerlifter and made time each day in his busy schedule to hit the gym. That's probably why he was able to fight off Lou Gehrig's disease for eight years.

Paul was a faithful attendee of my Wednesday-night men's Bible study at Stonebriar Community Church. When I first met Paul, he needed help to climb the stairs. Within a year he was in a wheelchair. Each night Paul would come rolling in with three or four friends. These guys would pick him up, load him into the Suburban, and then get him into his chair and wheel him into the study. Over the years, there were six or seven guys who would make sure that Paul made it to Bible study. They were very committed to Paul.

When Paul was diagnosed with ALS, he knew he was up against the biggest giant of his life. As any man would, he had great struggles with fear and anxiety—not so much over what would happen to him, but how his family would be taken care of while his body deteriorated. He was rapidly losing the ability to do anything for himself.

Instead of letting the giant master him, however, Paul started drawing closer to the Lord than he had ever been before. He began to study the

Scriptures in great depth. He was almost always at the Bible study—it was rare for him to ever miss. With a great hunger for the Word of God and the promises of God, he began to ask God to use this disease in his life for good. He was never content to sit on the sidelines, even as he lost the ability to control his body. He wanted to be used by God. He wanted God to use him even though his body was wasting away.

As a result of that determination, Paul began to write short essays for others who were suffering. The response was overwhelming, as many, many others dealing with different levels of brokenness in their lives gained courage from Paul's insights into the Scriptures. Eventually, with the help of Dave Turtletaub, one of his buddies who brought him to the study, Paul wrote a book on his struggle with ALS and the truths that he counted on to fight the giant disease.

As Paul's body grew steadily weaker, his inner man grew stronger. He wanted God to use him as long as there was breath in his body. Yes, he was serious about life, and about his approaching death. But that didn't keep him from a deep concern for those around him who didn't know Christ. He purposed in his heart that God would enable him to make a difference in the lives of others, instead of giving in to the giant of self-pity.

There were over a thousand people packed into the church for Paul's memorial service. It was one of those special services where Christ was honored, and Paul's impact on the lives of so many was celebrated. But it was at the end of the service when something remarkable took place. I went back to the serving area in the fellowship hall to get a glass of punch. Standing over in the corner were several of the guys who were part of Paul's Wednesday-night transportation team.

I went over to say hi. Now I have to tell you that I really didn't know most of these guys at all. I knew that several were doctors in the same practice with Paul, but that's about all. As we were talking about our mutual friend, one of the guys said, "Steve, I don't know how much you know about our group that would show up with Paul on Wednesday nights to Bible study, but you might find this interesting. It will give you a little insight into how Paul was always looking for a way to be used by the Lord.

"Not only did I work in the same medical practice as Paul, but I was his neighbor. I lived just a few blocks away. So when Paul was diagnosed with ALS, I told him to call anytime he needed some help. I was only a few minutes away and I wanted him to call on me. Over the next year or so, Paul called me several times to help him with some chores around the house that he couldn't quite do by himself anymore. And then one day I was over at the house, and he said, 'King, I've got a favor to ask.'

"'Sure, Paul,' I answered. 'Anything I can do I'm happy to do. How could I help you?'

"'I need you to help take me to my Bible study.'"

And that's when King told me, "Steve, I absolutely froze. I wasn't a Christian, wasn't a churchgoer, and I certainly didn't spend my time going to Bible studies. And Paul knew that. But he also knew that I desperately needed to find the Lord."

King continued the story: It took him a couple of seconds to get over his shock. He certainly wouldn't say no to Paul. King asked him how long the Bible study lasted, and Paul told him it was about an hour. King couldn't believe that someone would sit there for an hour studying the Bible. And then King asked Paul what he should do while Paul was in the study. Paul replied that he should just come in and sit with him. That way if Paul needed to go out for any reason, King could wheel him out.

King then told me that if he was going to go to this Bible study, he realized that he'd better go buy a Bible. So he went over to Barnes & Noble to get one. King told me that he couldn't believe there were so many different kinds of Bibles. He thought he would just walk in and grab a Bible. But there were Bible versions and translations from the floor to the ceiling. He was absolutely buffaloed by how many Bibles there were to choose from.

"Steve," he told me, "after nearly an hour of looking at all these different Bibles, I was completely lost. So finally I grabbed the New American Standard Bible. I figured I was a patriot and an American, and that I couldn't go wrong with a Bible that was all-American. That's how clueless I was five years ago when Paul invited me to help him get to the Bible study.

"And I was so worried about going to the Bible study that I began to read the Bible. Paul told me you guys were studying the book of Joshua. So the night before, I read the entire book of Joshua. I had never been to a Bible study in my life. But I figured the teacher might call on me and ask me a question. I didn't want to look like an idiot, so I read the whole book before I went to sleep.

"When I walked into that church the next night, I was really anxious. I told Paul I was pretty tired from staying up so late reading Joshua. He asked me why I did that, and I told him I was afraid that someone might call on me in class. He laughed and said, 'No, that won't happen. Steve just teaches, so you can sit there and relax.'"

King continued. "When I walked into that auditorium and saw several hundred guys, I was shocked. I figured there would be five or six guys sitting around a table. I was blown away that *that* many guys would show up on a Wednesday to study the Bible. I figured I would be bored to tears, but I wasn't. I wasn't even sure that I believed in the Bible. But before long the Holy Spirit began to work in my heart, and I began to see that I was a sinner and that my only hope was to believe the gospel of Christ. And within the year, my life was completely changed by the Lord.

"Paul knew that I needed to find the Lord, and he also knew that he had me when I had offered to do anything I could for him. I never thought it would mean taking him to Bible study, especially since he already had three other guys helping him. Even in his increasing weakness, Paul was looking for ways to be used by God. And I am the product of his unwillingness to just stay home and be defeated by self-pity."

We all stood around and had a good laugh about Paul's evangelistic strategy. And then one of the other guys, Larry, whom I hadn't seen in a couple of years, said, "Steve, do you know of any books that I could share with some Hindu doctors that I work with?"

"I didn't know you had any Hindu doctors in your practice."

"Well, I'm not in Paul's practice anymore. I have a unique specialty, and I moved out of state about two years ago. But I'm the only Christian and the rest of the doctors are Hindus."

"Are they open to the gospel?"

"A couple of them are more open than I was when I showed up at the Bible study for the first time."

"When was that?"

"Well, I started coming about five years ago. Paul worked the same thing on me that he worked on King. I was an atheist. And I was a very committed atheist. But the next thing I knew, I was taking Paul to your Bible study and sitting there for an hour listening to you teach things I didn't believe. And within a year I came to know the Lord. He came into my life and completely turned me into a new man. I went from unbelief to belief so fast I couldn't believe it. And neither could my family. But Paul knew that I needed the Lord whom I had denied. And Paul was the human instrument that God used to bring me to salvation. I wouldn't have gone to a Bible study for anyone else on the face of the earth. But Paul knew that I would do it for him."

Is this the script that Paul had planned for his life when he was twenty-one? Obviously not. But when this giant of ALS came into his life, Paul fought it with everything he had. He displayed strength even as he became weak and did great exploits that radically changed the lives of at least two men and their families.

But don't miss this.

It happened because Paul knew God.

He knew His character, His power, His wisdom—and all of the other attributes of God that we mentioned earlier in this chapter. He wrote a book for suffering people that is all about the greatness of God. Paul didn't waste his life. He didn't get stupid and panic. He didn't deny his God, and he didn't run from the giant. He hated the giant of losing his life early—but he knew that God was in control of all things. And that kept him going.

Paul had guts. He had gravitas. His life remains an example of what it means to be a man who was used by God.

When I think of leaders with character, I immediately think of Joshua and Caleb. And then you have to throw in Samuel Adams and John Hancock. John Wycliffe is right in there with them with his burned bones and ashes floating around somewhere in the Gulf of Mexico. And I would throw Paul Lanier's name into the mix as well.

A leader with character. Those are the guys who God uses to fight the giants—and bring honor to His name.

Chapter Four

Slaves

"A nation has character only when it is free."
—*De Stael*

J oshua and Caleb were born slaves.

We see them as men of faith and battle, and they were. But it was the slavery and suffering that put the iron in their souls.

They started their lives as slaves. Their fathers were slaves and so were their grandfathers. For hundreds of years the men of Israel were slaves in Egypt.

You've got to look backward to see a man's background. But when you understand a man's background, you better understand the man. As the Lord declared in the book of Isaiah: "Look to the rock from which you were hewn and to the quarry from which you were dug" (51:1 NASB).

Joshua and Caleb were hewn out of a quarry called slavery, and it marked their lives. That was also the case with missionary pioneer David Livingstone: His background helps explain his character.

David Livingstone was not one to be caged indoors. This great ambassador of Jesus Christ roamed Africa and went where no white man had ever gone before. He walked thousands of miles across that continent, preaching the gospel and doing all he could do to expose and extinguish the extensive slave trade.

After ten years of ministry in South Africa he had only one

convert—and that man eventually left Christianity and embraced his old ways of polygamy. Livingstone was crushed and frustrated. He had stayed too long in one place with nothing to show for his efforts. The small town was too confining for the man who had been confined throughout his childhood.

He then began to make some of the most dangerous and courageous explorations of the nineteenth century.[1] He explored twelve African countries, and his personal goal was to open a fifteen-hundred-mile trail into the interior of Africa to bring "Christianity and civilization" to unreached people.[2]

Livingstone's life is best understood by two factors: his vision for the people of Africa at an early age, and his laboring as a boy in slave-like conditions. When he was just a young lad in Scotland, he heard a preacher by the name of Robert Moffatt speak of seeing "the smoke of a thousand villages" who had never heard the gospel of Christ.[3] It became the dream of young Livingstone to become a medical doctor, visit those thousand villages, and give to them the good news about Christ. But if anyone ever had the odds against them of pursuing their dream, it was David Livingstone. His parents were godly people, yet extremely poor. David lived in a one-room house with his parents and five brothers and sisters. It was all his father could do to make ends meet and put food on the table.

"At the age of ten he went to work in the cotton factory as a piecer, and after some years was promoted to be a spinner. The first half-crown he earned he gave to his mother. With part of his first week's wages he bought a Latin textbook and studied that language with ardor in an evening class between eight and ten. He had to be in the factory at six in the morning, and his work ended at eight at night. But by working at Latin until midnight he mastered Virgil and Horace by the time he was sixteen. He used to read in the factory by putting the book on the spinning jenny so that he could catch a sentence at a time as he passed at his work. He was fond of botany and geology and zoology, and when he could get out would scour the country for specimens."[4]

A young piecer like Livingstone did brutal work. "They had to be unusually agile since their work often involved climbing under the machinery or balancing over it. Piecers walked anything up to twenty miles a day in the mills, and much of this distance was covered in crawling or stooping positions. Long hours on their feet often led to the development of bow legs and varicose veins ... many of the children would end up with limbs deformed and growth stunted."[5]

Day after day he worked away in the cramped and confined space, spinning the cotton and mentally disciplining himself to glimpse a sentence at a time out of his Latin book. As he worked and drilled himself with Latin, he somehow managed to keep his dream alive: It was in his heart to become a missionary doctor. But first he had to get out of the mill and get in to college. And frankly, that goal seemed impossible.

Livingstone's situation at work was nothing less than horrific. Today such conditions are considered unlawful. Livingstone was paid a small wage for his work, but nevertheless had to endure brutally long hours of labor in cramped, confined sweatshop conditions.

He wasn't a slave, but he worked in slavelike conditions. And the suffering of that near slavery put iron in his soul.

After spending his childhood in the cotton mill, no wonder he flourished in the wide-open spaces of Africa. In conditions that would make strong men lose their health, Livingstone kept walking, thousands and thousands of miles. He wasn't confined to a dark, noisy mill anymore. He had the freedom to go where he needed to go and to explore lands that no one from the Western world had ever seen. He was fulfilling the dream of his childhood, and he was grateful for the opportunities that God had brought his way.

In this, he was very similar to Joshua and Caleb. He had been set free from a confining life, and so had they.

Childhood Slavery

Some men have great pedigrees and bloodlines.

Joshua was a great man and a great leader, but he was seriously lacking in the pedigree department. Phillip Keller observed that "he [Joshua] has seldom been given the full credit he deserves as perhaps the greatest man of faith ever to set foot on the stage of human history. In fact, his entire brilliant career was a straightforward story of simply setting down one foot after another in quiet compliance with the commands of God."[6]

Pedigree? He was a slave, and the son and grandson of slaves. That was his lineage and his start in life. Herbert Lockyer gives a summary of Joshua's less-than-glamorous beginnings:

> Born during the weary years of bondage his nation suffered in
> Egypt under Pharaoh, Joshua knew something of the lash of
> the whip, the almost impossible tasks in the brick-fields, and
> the deep sigh of liberty. But little did he realize that although
> a slave, he would rise to become Israel's supreme leader and
> commander.[7]

When a man is a slave, he will find himself fighting four significant giants:

- A life of few or no results
- A scenario of unfulfilled dreams
- A daily experience of physical and emotional exhaustion
- A future with few or no prospects

Quite frankly, that is what David Livingstone faced in the cotton mill, and it is what Joshua experienced as a young man slaving away in Egypt. No results ... unfulfilled dreams ... physical and emotional exhaustion ... a future with few or no prospects.

That may be what you are feeling and experiencing in your own life right now.

But you say, "I'm not a slave."

Nevertheless, if you live in America, you *are* a slave—you just don't realize it. You have become an economic slave, and it is affecting your entire life. And you have to come to grips with it every time you fill up your car.

In 1973, the United States imported about 24 percent of our oil. In 1990, we were dependent on foreign nations for 42 percent of our oil. And in 2008, we were importing nearly 70 percent of our oil.

I'm sure you have seen the TV commercials that Texas oilman Boone Pickens has been airing across the nation. Pickens recently wrote a disturbing opinion piece in the *Wall Street Journal* about our predicament.

> This year we will spend almost $700 billion on imported oil, which is more than four times the annual cost of our war in Iraq.
>
> In fact, if we don't do anything about this problem, over the next ten years we will spend around $10 trillion importing foreign oil. That is $10 trillion leaving the U.S. and going to foreign nations, making it what I certainly believe will be the single largest transfer of wealth in human history.
>
> Why do I believe that our dependence on foreign oil is such a danger to our country? Put simply, our economic engine is now 70 percent dependent on the energy

resources of other countries, their good judgment, and most importantly, their goodwill toward us.[8]

Pickens didn't come out and actually say this, but allow me to say it: We have become slaves.

When we are 70 percent dependent for oil on other countries, and their good judgment (which is questionable at best), and their goodwill (which is also highly questionable and could turn on a dime), there is just one word for someone in those circumstances: *slave*.

I'm writing this on December 8, 2008. Yesterday I filled up my truck and paid $1.49 a gallon. But this past summer, everybody in America was paying $4 a gallon.

So, what do you think? Is the price of gas going to stay below a buck-fifty a gallon from here on out? I don't believe that, and I doubt that you do either. We have great untapped oil resources in our nation, but for whatever reason, those potential oil fields have been declared sacred and off-limits. So we're dependent on other nations that have the oil. And that's what scared Winston Churchill about oil in the first place.

In 1911, Winston Churchill was First Lord of the Admiralty and faced a monumental decision. "The issue was whether to convert the British Navy to oil in place of coal. Many thought that such a conversion was pure folly, for it meant that the Navy could no longer rely on safe, Welsh coal, but rather would have to depend on distant and insecure oil supplies from Persia, as Iran was then known.

"To commit the Navy irrevocably to oil was indeed to 'take arms against a sea of troubles,' said Churchill. But the strategic benefits—great speed and more efficient use of manpower—were so obvious to him that he did not dally. He decided that Britain would have to base its 'naval supremacy upon oil' and thereupon, committed himself, with all his driving energy and enthusiasm, to achieving that objective.

"There was no choice. In Churchill's words, 'Mastery itself was the prize of the venture.'"[9]

And when it comes to oil, if one is not a master, one is a slave.

Back in 1911, Churchill knew full well the essence of the gamble. Great Britain had enough coal within its borders to last a thousand years, but it would have to search elsewhere for mastery over a reliable oil supply. And for decades, they had such mastery of vast oil reserves in the Middle East. But then the tables turned. And Great Britain and the United States are no longer masters.

We are now slaves.

Oil is the lifeblood of American life, but others control the spigot and the price. We don't control the oil—it controls us. And that's an economic giant that affects all of us. We were all feeling the pinch at $4 a gallon, so I must say it was sure nice to see that pump at $1.49. But for some reason I have a sneaking suspicion that we will see $4 again in the future. And if it can hit $4, why couldn't it hit $5 or even $6 somewhere down the road?

After all, we're just the slaves—somebody else a half a world away is setting the price.

Prophetic on Oil

Daniel Yergin was prophetic when he wrote the following in 1993:

> Today, we are so dependent on oil, and oil is so embedded
> in our daily doings, that we hardly stop to comprehend its
> pervasive significance. It is oil that makes possible where
> we live, how we commute to work, how we travel—even
> where we conduct our courtships. It is the lifeblood of
> suburban communities. Oil (and natural gas) are the

essential components in the fertilizer on which world
agriculture depends; oil makes it possible to transport
food to the totally non-self-sufficient mega cities of the
world. Oil also provides the plastics and chemicals that
are the bricks and mortar of contemporary civilization,
a civilization that would collapse if the world's oil wells
suddenly went dry.[10]

Or if someone in Venezuela or the Middle East turned off the tap. Of if
the leftist earth worshippers in Congress continue to halt drilling. It could
all collapse—or just continue to deteriorate into greater economic chaos.

Now you may be thinking, *Hey, Farrar, I didn't buy this book to read
about the economic crisis, people losing their jobs, and the price of oil going
crazy. I want God to use me.*

May I throw out something for you to consider?

As more and more people are squeezed and frightened by economic
difficulties and chaos, as more and more people are laid off and lose their
homes, as more and more people simply try to survive these new hard
times, don't you think that many of the people will begin to realize they
need something bigger than themselves? Don't you think that people who
haven't thought of God in the good times might be looking for Him out of
desperation in the lean times?

It's in those anxious and fearful economic conditions that God will
be raising up men that He can use. And you're one of them. Listen to the
wisdom of Dr. Martyn Lloyd-Jones:

We are all being watched at the present time. The world
is most unhappy, men and women do not know what to
do, and they do not know where to turn. When they see
someone who seems to be calm and steadfast, someone

who is not utterly bewildered at a time like this, someone
who seems to have an insight into it all, and who can
look beyond it all, they look and say, "What is this? What
is this person's secret?" And so you become an evangelist
by just standing and being 'strong in the Lord, and in
the power of His might.' You are not carried away by the
flood, you do not do things because everyone else is doing
them, you have principles of your own, and you are ready
to stand for them and to suffer for them. That has often
been the means, under God's blessing, of awakening others and convicting them of sin, and causing them to begin
to enquire after God.[11]

That's a great description of how God can use you when things around
you are breaking down. You see, when people are overwhelmed and frightened of the giants of stagflation or inflation or deflation, they need to see
someone who isn't. And the person who can face those giants and have
peace in days of economic uncertainty is the man whom God will use to
point others to Jesus Christ.

If you have trusted Christ as your only hope for salvation (Rom.
10:9–10), you should know that, in reality, you are *not* an economic
slave. You are a son of the living God, and therefore you have a preferred
status in this world. Your Father has His eye on you. He knows where
you are, He knows all of your needs, and He has pledged to meet those
needs—simply because you belong to Him. That's certainly how I read
Romans 8:32:

He who did not spare his own Son but gave him up for
us all, how will he not also with him graciously give us all
things?

Sons, Not Slaves

If Christ is your Lord and Savior, then you are not a slave.

Nor are you an owner.

That last one may surprise you. Of course we're owners! You own a house, a couple of cars, some stock....

It's true that you may look like an owner. But what you really are is a steward. It is God who owns it all. He has simply entrusted a certain amount of money and property into your care and oversight for a season. It really isn't yours; it's His. And sometimes He takes it away to get our attention.

The December 6, 2008, edition of *The Economist* carried a cheery little article titled "Where Have All Your Savings Gone?" Here is a short clip that will undoubtedly remind you that you are not an owner:

> For American and European savers it has been a lost decade. After two booms and two busts, stock markets have earned them nothing, or less, in the past ten years.... As a result, saving seems like pouring money into a black hole. Any American who has diligently put $100 into a domestic equity mutual fund for the past ten years will find his pot worth less than he put into it.

I was reading this morning in George Müller's autobiography about a letter he received from an Irish businessman.[12] The man had been giving to Müller's orphanage for approximately four years. In the letter the man stated that he had been very confused about giving, but reading Müller's pamphlets had helped him tremendously. Over the last four years he apparently had grabbed on to Müller's emphasis that each man is a steward instead of an owner. This man began to realize that what he had been given was really the Lord's, and that he was responsible to use his money wisely. Gradually, he began to give more than he had before. When he saw a need, he would use his funds to help meet the need. Interestingly enough, the more he gave the more he was given. Every time he would give to meet someone's need, he would almost immediately see a larger amount come his way.

I bring this up for a reason.

In his letter to Müller this man mentions that even in the midst of the bank panic of 1857, he continued to give as the Lord led him. He didn't worry about the external factors that were causing such anxiety. He just followed the leading of the Lord and continued to give to those who were in need as he was able. And even as other men in his line of manufacturing faced financial ruin, he continued to see an increase in his business. He not only had enough to take care of his family, but to help out many others as well.

So here we are smack in the middle of a bank and financial panic, and we have the same God that this man had. He understood that he was not an owner. He was a steward. And he understood Luke 6:38: "Give, and it will be given to you."

If God is your Father through Jesus Christ His Son, then you don't need to panic about Fannie Mae, the Federal Reserve, or the price of oil.

Why? Because you're not only a steward—you're a *son*. And your Father knows that you need all these things (Matt. 6:32). So seek Him first—not sixth, not third. Seek Him first, and He will work it all out for you. Even in the midst of a financial meltdown (Matt. 6:33–34).

Several weeks ago I had coffee with a man who has been a part of the Wednesday-night study for maybe five years. As we were talking, he told me that when he first started coming to the Bible study, he really didn't take Christianity too seriously. But then the Lord really got hold of his heart and his mind, and it started affecting his entire life. He told me that maybe four years ago I had taught on giving, and for the first time, he began to think about giving to the Lord.

This was all new to him, and he was somewhat confused on how to begin. And then he said, "Steve, do you remember a few weeks ago talking about that Irish businessman who wrote the letter to George Müller? That guy was telling my story. He said that when he got frightened about giving and withdrew, God withdrew the money from his business. But whenever he would give, the money would start flowing back into his business. That's been my experience, Steve. And do you remember him talking about the year of the big financial panic? He said that a lot of other businesses in his field were failing. Steve, it's really something to watch. Here we are in all of this financial turmoil, and I've got competitors who are going down. But I have continued to increase my giving, and I'm having the best year I've ever had."

And then he said, "By the way, do you know anyone who has a serious financial need?"

I replied, "As a matter of fact I do." I told him of a single mom who was in desperate straits. After I gave him a few details, he asked, "Would you mind coming by my house when we leave here? I've got something I'd like for you to give her for me—but please don't tell her my name."

The next day I saw the single mom, and she told me that her employer had let her go. He had asked her to lie to some customers, and she refused. She fought back the tears as she told me the story.

I listened, and then I said, "Well, I know that is deeply disappointing, but I also want you to know that I believe that God will honor you for telling the truth. I know you needed that income, and God knows that. But I'm convinced He is going to honor you. In fact, He's going to honor you right now."

And that's when I pulled out the envelope that I had been given the night before and gave it to her. "There's two thousand dollars in that envelope. The Lord put it on someone's heart last night to give it to you. They want to remain anonymous, but it's very important to them that you know it's from the Lord."

I wish I could describe to you the look on her face.

She was almost as thrilled as the man who gave me the envelope.

Joshua's Slavery Biography

When it comes to details of Joshua's life as a slave, we have absolutely nothing to go on. The Bible never mentions his early life or gives us any insights into the pressure and difficulty of his immediate family situation. We don't have a clue about what he personally went through as a young slave in Egypt.

But we do know this: There was a shame in being a slave and deep humiliation as well. If a man is found in any kind of slavery—be it physical, sexual, emotional, or economic—he will inevitably have to wrestle with some shame and humiliation.

Joshua was born and raised a slave. But even though we don't have any details or stories of his early life as we do of Joseph and Daniel (who were also slaves in their early years), we certainly know three things about Joshua:

- Slavery marked him.
- Slavery haunted him.
- Slavery prepared him.

Joshua was a man who was greatly used by God. You want to be used and so do I. So we must understand something of the process that God takes a man through in order to get him ready for his assignment. Oswald Sanders comments with his usual insight:

> It is usually God's method to bring a leader into promi-
> nence only slowly. As A. W. Tozer remarked, God rarely

projects His chosen servants to suddenly burst upon the world without previous preparation. [Most] will be found to have spent a long apprenticeship to God somewhere before being entrusted with important work.[13]

A man who desires to be used by God will be apprenticed and trained in difficult circumstances. Romans 5:1–5 (NKJV) states it very clearly:

> Therefore, having been justified by faith, we have peace with God through our Lord Jesus Christ, through whom also we have access by faith into this grace in which we stand, and rejoice in hope of the glory of God. And not only that, but we also glory in tribulations, knowing that tribulation produces perseverance; and perseverance, character; and character, hope. Now hope does not disappoint, because the love of God has been poured out in our hearts by the Holy Spirit who was given to us.

How in the world do we rejoice in our sufferings?

We rejoice by knowing. (And by the way, here we are once again having to *think*.) What are we to know? When Paul says "knowing," he's simply challenging you to think about what's going on in your life. I like the insight of John J. Murray:

> The process by which God builds character is outlined in Romans 5:1–5. Paul says that "we glory in tribulation." The Greek word translated "tribulation" comes from the verb "to press." The word is used to describe the crushing of grapes and olives. The figure suggests the heavy pressures of outward trouble or inward anguish. Tribulation

produces "patient endurance"—the ability to stay with it
and not fall apart.[14]

Joshua and Caleb had character. And why did they have character?
Because they had suffered as slaves—pressed hard and crushed as young
men. When you're a slave, you have outward trouble and inward anguish.
But God is in your suffering, and He brings the hardship for a reason!

You're not suffering by accident or by chance; you are suffering according to the will of God:

> Therefore, those also who suffer according to the will of
> God shall entrust their souls to a faithful Creator in doing
> what is right. (1 Peter 4:19 NASB)

Like a spiritual trainer, He is developing spiritual muscle in your inner
man (Eph. 2:10). And the way that He gets you ready to be used is by
suffering that produces endurance—and by endurance that produces character. And because you understand that you can't be used with a fatally
flawed character, you don't lose hope as you go through this process.

Bone Crushing

That's doesn't mean it's easy. In fact, it's hard at times. Maybe even bone crushing. But you are *not* suffering by chance, rotten luck, or bad karma. Overseeing
your entire life, God will use the suffering and the difficulties to get you ready
for the work He has for you to do. He did that with Joshua, and He will do it
for you. He *will* use you—and the suffering and hardship is evidence—biblical
evidence—that this is the very thing He has in mind for you.

That may mean that as things get tough economically in our nation, you may feel the squeeze. You may feel the pressure. Economic hardship is a giant running loose in our land right now, and this is a giant who's feeling his oats. He hasn't been this active since the mid 1970s—or perhaps even the 1930s.

This may be a giant in your life that you never counted on. But tell me this: Isn't it possible that God would use your battle with this giant to put some iron into your soul, teaching you to trust Him and find Him faithful as never before?

That is the path to being used by God. I'm neither a prophet nor the son of a prophet, so I can't say for sure what will or won't happen to you and your family in the coming days. You may feel an economic pinch that you never expected or anticipated. But if you do, it will be under the careful oversight of your heavenly Father.

Even so, you may not like those conditions. Remember how we described the hardships in the life of a slave?

- A life of few or no results
- A scenario of unfulfilled dreams
- A daily experience of physical and emotional exhaustion
- A future with few or no prospects

You may or may not see giants like these poke their ugly heads up over your economic horizon in this season of your life. But let me give you a little encouragement. God has *not* planned a life for you of few or no results. He has a work for you to do, and frankly, you can't die until you accomplish it (see Eph. 2:10).

Even so, you may go through a period of time when you see few or no results to prepare you for the work that God has ahead of you. You may lose your dreams for a while or become physically and emotionally exhausted just trying to make ends meet. And you may look out at your future and not see any prospects for your situation to change. But to lose hope would be a very big mistake. God uses seasons of barrenness and hardship to prepare men for fruitfulness and influence.

J. C. Ryle is a man who proves that point.

From Riches to Rags

J. C. Ryle? Wasn't he a wide receiver out of Alabama back in '71?

As a matter of fact, he wasn't.

You've heard of rags to riches? J. C. Ryle went from riches to rags—and it factored in to God's plans to use him.

Ryle was 6'3" and 220 pounds, but he didn't play football. In the 1840s, he was captain of the cricket teams at Eton and then Oxford. This guy had it all—money, brains, good looks, and that tremendous hand-eye coordination that every great athlete is born with. He was a golden boy. But his life took a little bit of a turn shortly after he graduated with honors from Oxford. He became what we describe today as an assistant pastor in a little church in rural England. And it didn't work out quite like he had envisioned.

J. C. Ryle eventually became the first Anglican bishop of Liverpool, England. But unlike many Anglican bishops, he was a thoroughgoing, Bible-believing pastor. He worked tirelessly among the lower classes of Liverpool, preaching the Word, establishing schools, and generally improving their lot by preaching the gospel. But at the age of twenty-five, he had no plans of pastoral work. He had set his sights on Parliament. But his father's shocking bankruptcy changed everything.

Ryle had entered this world as a child of privilege, born into an extremely wealthy family. His father was a silk merchant and a banker, and the magnificent family home was situated on a thousand acres with a full array of servants. Both a brilliant student and a gifted leader at the tender age of twenty-five, Ryle was financially set for life and ready to enter Parliament.

And then in one day's time, everything changed.

In an autobiography that he wrote when he was fifty-seven for his children to read after his death, Ryle describes it in his own words:

> My father was a wealthy man. He was a landed proprietor and a banker. I was the eldest son and looked forward to inheriting a large fortune. I was on the point of entering Parliament. I had all things before me until I was twenty-five. But it then pleased God to alter my prospects in life through my father's bankruptcy. We got up one summer's morning with all the world before us as usual and went to bed that evening completely and entirely ruined.
>
> It would perhaps be impossible to give any correct idea of the stunning violence of the blow, which the ruin inflicted upon all.... The immediate consequences were bitter and painful in the extreme, and humiliating to the utmost degree. The creditors naturally rightly and justly seized everything and we children were left with nothing but our own personal property and our clothes.... Our household, of course, was immediately broken up—menservants, butler, underbutler, footman, coachman, groom, housekeeper, housemaids.[15]

Henbury, the family's majestic one-thousand-acre family home, was sold, and life as Ryle had known it for all of his twenty-five years was over. And so was his future. He had become a Christian just the year before, and little did he know that in six months he would find himself in the position of an assistant pastor. But of course, he had no idea of how God planned to use him. All he could see was the utter ruin and humiliation.

With all the world before me [I] lost everything and saw the whole future of my life, turned upside down and thrown into confusion. If I hadn't been a Christian at that time, I do not know if I should not have committed suicide. As it was, everybody said how beautifully I behaved, how resigned I was, what an example of contentment I was. Never was there more a complete mistake. God alone knows how the iron entered into my soul; how my whole frame—body, mind and spirit—reeled and was shaken to the foundation under the blow of my father's ruin. I am quite certain it inflicted a wound on my body and mind, of which I feel the effects most heavily at this day and shall feel it if I live to be a hundred. To suppose that people do not feel things because they do not scream and yell and fill the air with their cries is simple nonsense.

The plain fact was there was no one of the family whom it touched more than it did me. My father and mother were no longer young and in the downhill of life; my brothers and sisters, of course, never expected to live at Henbury [their family home] and naturally never thought of it as their house after a certain time. I, on the contrary, as the eldest son, twenty-five, with all the world before me, lost everything, and saw the whole future of my life turned upside down and thrown into confusion.

I do not think that there has ever been a single day in my life for thirty years that I have not remembered the great humiliation of having to leave Henbury. During that thirty-two years I have lived in many houses and been in many positions. I have always tried to make the best of them and to be cheerful in every circumstance, but

nothing has made me forget my sudden violent expul-
sion from Cheshire in 1841.... Ever since I left Cheshire
I have never felt at home, but a sojourner and a dweller
in a lodging.[16]

The humiliation that Ryle felt is hard for us to imagine. But in a class-
rigid society such as Victorian England, his father's financial failure was
the ultimate disgrace. Ryle was completely humiliated. He had literally
overnight not only lost his fortune, but also his friends, his social standing,
and his occupational plans for the future. Through no fault of his own, he
had become a complete and total outcast, falling from the peak of British
society to the very bottom. His former servants were in better shape than
he was. He was living in absolute poverty:

I never felt before what a miserable thing it is for a man
to be first rich and then poor.... Those only who have
been rich till they were twenty-five, and then become
poor can comprehend what endless mortification your
circumstances entail upon you.[17]
God never expects us to feel no suffering or pain when
it pleases Him to visit us with affliction. There are great
mistakes upon this point. Submission to God's will is perfectly compatible with intense and keen suffering under
the chastisement of His will. Troubles in fact not felt are
not troubles at all. To feel trouble deeply and yet submit to
it patiently is what is required of a Christian.... I ask my
children and everyone who may read this autobiography to
remember that I felt most acutely my father's ruin, my exile
from Cheshire with destruction of all my worldly property
and I have never ceased to feel them from that day to this;

but I would have them know that I was submissive to God's will and had a firm and deep conviction that all was right, though I could not see it or feel it at the time.[18]

The bankruptcy marked him.

The bankruptcy haunted him.

The bankruptcy *prepared* him—for a life of service and fruitfulness that he never could have imagined.

At the age of sixty-five, just as he made plans to downshift a little bit and take on less strenuous responsibilities, the position in Liverpool was offered to him. It was a monumental task in a seaport town, with many poor and destitute people. For the next twenty years, he did a magnificent work among the lower classes. They felt like the Oxford-educated man understood them. And understand them he did. The fortunate ones were servants, but the majority of them lived at the poverty level. He understood their poverty because he had experienced it. And God had used it for Ryle's good, the good of the people, and for His own glory.

A man who says to God, "Use me," will go through a rough process. Don't let anyone kid you about that. God is a good God, but He knows that we need to go through boot camp before we can be the men that we truly desire to become.

That's why a leader is …

- tested before he is trusted;
- seasoned before he is successful;
- prepared before he is promoted;
- refined before he is ready.

That's what happened to Ryle, and it was certainly Joshua's experience as well. You can find it in the life of any godly man whom God picks up and uses. Suffering is part of the Christian life. It is taught throughout the Scriptures that suffering is for our benefit and endurance, and that we are honed to a sharp edge in adversity. That's why John Gere, a Puritan pastor who had known great suffering in the cause of Christ, stated that "he who suffers conquers."

It could very well be that we are about to face some times of intense economic suffering. It may be that some of us will see a reversal in our economic fortunes. Economically, those four giants of …

- a life of few or no results;
- a scenario of unfulfilled dreams;
- a daily experience of physical and emotional exhaustion;
- a future with few or no prospects

may become very real to some, if not all of us.

But if such days truly do come our way, it will be because our faithful God is preparing us to do a great work. And there's no reason to fear the future or become anxious.

It was Martin Luther, a man who knew much of suffering and much of being used for God's glory, who penned these words: "Our Lord God resembles a typesetter, who sets his letters backward. We definitely see and feel that He is setting His type, but the print we shall see in the beyond. Meanwhile we must have patience."

To understand Joshua and Caleb, one has to look backward.

To understand Livingstone and Ryle, one must again look backward.

Your suffering may be in the present—but before long you will only see it backward. May He give you the patience to know that He is at work—and that He can be trusted to use it to put iron in your soul.

Chapter Five

Increased Hardship

*"It is said that in some countries trees will grow,
but will bear no fruit, because there is no winter there."*
—*John Bunyan*

From time to time I'm asked if I have any hobbies.

I'll be honest with you, that's a frustrating question for me.

I can tell you all the reasons why I *should* have a hobby, a pastime, or some relaxing diversion that I particularly enjoy, but the fact is, I don't.

So I always respond by telling the person that I am, in all candor, somewhat of a boring person. I don't golf, do woodworking, or hang out in a greenhouse.

Now, I'm not saying that's a good thing.

I'm sure a hobby would be a positive thing to have, and would help me to relax. But I have no idea what it would be. I don't restore classic cars, do archery, collect antiques, or raise Labrador retrievers. In other words, no, I don't have a hobby.

Or … at least not in the expected, traditional sense.

But I recently had a significant revelation that maybe I do have a hobby of sorts. And the fact is, I've been enjoying this hobby since I was seven years old.

I read biographies.

Now, a hobby like that might not ring your chimes. I can appreciate that. But it helps me to realize that maybe I really do have an enjoyable pastime—something I do for fun. I like to read the story of a person's life. When I was a kid, I started reading biographies of famous athletes—guys like Babe Ruth and Mickey Mantle. For over fifty years, I've been reading biographies.

I read biographies for the same reason that A. W. N. Pugin sketched and drew buildings when he was a kid. Pugin was the greatest British architect of the nineteenth century. "One building stands above all others as a testament to Pugin's influence. *The Palace of Westminster* (i.e., The Houses of Parliament) in London, was built under the direction of Sir Charles Barry, but Pugin was responsible for every aspect of the interiors, as well as for creating working drawings of all the exterior details."[1] It was a staggering achievement. But Pugin didn't begin by just jumping in and designing buildings—he began by sketching them.

Pugin started drawing at the age of three, and would take annual trips in the summer with his father for the purpose of drawing the great buildings of Europe. He stated,

> "The way to understand architecture thoroughly is to draw buildings, with care and in great detail. You are obliged to look at a building closely, repeatedly, and for long periods. Only thus do you learn what the architect was doing in a particular case, and as a rule you are also able to identify the contributions of the masons, carpenters, and other craftsmen...."
>
> [Pugin's] close study and reproduction on paper of actual medieval creations were the key to designing his own, and helped him to enter the minds of medieval builders and decorators: they formed, as it were, his apprenticeship

under experts who had lived hundreds of years before him, until he became a master mason himself.[2]

Now reading a passage like that might not cause your pulse to quicken at all, but it absolutely fires me up. I get inspired. I read biographies of men in particular because I want to observe how it is that God fashions and makes men. And when I read a biography, I see the providential hand of God at work in the life of a man, no matter if he is a great general, a power-hungry politician, or an introverted nerd who came up with some great invention. In the life of every man there are great lessons to be learned of the work of God—but you have to observe very closely. God's providential hand is constantly at work in the lives of men. And observing that divine activity gives us significant clues on how God will work in building our lives.

I've noticed something about biographies. It's safe to say that nearly every person that I have read about has at some point in his or her life faced a period of sharply increased hardship. I'm not talking about the normal cares and difficulties of life. What I have in mind is an intensified, increased hardship that is so fraught with pressure that it threatens to pulverize the man. And when a man encounters that kind of increased hardship, it either makes him—or breaks him.

This is what happened at a certain point to Joshua and Caleb.

And it will happen to you.

Straw

"The straw that broke the camel's back."

I've heard that phrase all of my life and so have you. Allow me to introduce you to the straw that broke the back of the men of Israel. And you

might want to give it your undivided attention, because we all may be in
the same position economically before long. You can find the explanation
in Exodus 5, but it's important to understand the context.

The children of Israel are slaves, as we looked at in the last chapter.
Joshua and Caleb are slaves. But out of nowhere, Moses shows up after
spending forty years in the wilderness with a simple message for Pharaoh:
"God says that you are to let the people go."

And then he has a message for all of the Israelite slaves: "God is about
to deliver you." That's the context. Now watch what happens in Exodus 5:

> Afterward Moses and Aaron went and said to Pharaoh,
> "Thus says the LORD, the God of Israel, 'Let my people go,
> that they may hold a feast to me in the wilderness.'" But
> Pharaoh said, "Who is the LORD, that I should obey his
> voice and let Israel go? I do not know the LORD, and more-
> over, I will not let Israel go." Then they said, "The God of
> the Hebrews has met with us. Please let us go a three days'
> journey into the wilderness that we may sacrifice to the
> LORD our God, lest he fall upon us with pestilence or with
> the sword." But the king of Egypt said to them, "Moses and
> Aaron, why do you take the people away from their work?
> Get back to your burdens." And Pharaoh said, "Behold, the
> people of the land are now many, and you make them rest
> from their burdens!" The same day Pharaoh commanded
> the taskmasters of the people and their foremen, "You
> shall no longer give the people straw to make bricks, as in
> the past; let them go and gather straw for themselves. But
> the number of bricks that they made in the past you shall
> impose on them, you shall by no means reduce it, for they
> are idle. Therefore they cry, 'Let us go and offer sacrifice to

our God.' Let heavier work be laid on the men that they may labor at it and pay no regard to lying words."

So the taskmasters and the foremen of the people went out and said to the people, "Thus says Pharaoh, 'I will not give you straw. Go and get your straw yourselves wherever you can find it, but your work will not be reduced in the least.'" So the people were scattered throughout all the land of Egypt to gather stubble for straw. The taskmasters were urgent, saying, "Complete your work, your daily task each day, as when there was straw." And the foremen of the people of Israel, whom Pharaoh's taskmasters had set over them, were beaten and were asked, "Why have you not done all your task of making bricks today and yesterday, as in the past?"

Then the foremen of the people of Israel came and cried to Pharaoh, "Why do you treat your servants like this? No straw is given to your servants, yet they say to us, 'Make bricks!' And behold, your servants are beaten; but the fault is in your own people." But he said, "You are idle, you are idle; that is why you say, 'Let us go and sacrifice to the LORD.' Go now and work. No straw will be given you, but you must still deliver the same number of bricks." The foremen of the people of Israel saw that they were in trouble when they said, "You shall by no means reduce your number of bricks, your daily task each day." They met Moses and Aaron, who were waiting for them, as they came out from Pharaoh; and they said to them, "The LORD look on you and judge, because you have made us stink in the sight of Pharaoh and his servants, and have put a sword in their hand to kill us."

Then Moses turned to the LORD and said, "O LORD, why have you done evil to this people? Why did you ever send me? For since I came to Pharaoh to speak in your name, he has done evil to this people, and you have not delivered your people at all."

These slaves were already grappling the four giants that we mentioned earlier. And what were they again? They were fighting the giants of ...

- a life of few or no results;
- a scenario of unfulfilled dreams;
- a daily experience of physical and emotional exhaustion;
- a future with little or no prospects.

At this point, Joshua and Caleb are just anonymous men—like all of the other men of Israel who are slaves. Joshua and Caleb and all of the other men, along with their families, are living a dull and monotonous existence—and life is pretty tough. And now, in addition to these four giants, they are suddenly fighting one more. Some giants are bigger than others and this new one is a monster. This one is *the giant of increased hardship*.

This giant was the straw that broke the camel's back. That's not quite right, because they took the straw *off* the camel's back and put it on the backs of the men of Israel. And they were already physically and emotionally exhausted.

So let's get this straight. Moses shows up and says to these guys that God has sent me to deliver you. But Pharaoh gets hacked off and says not only am I not going to let you go, but I'm going to fire the subcontractors who bring the straw to you. So not only do you have to produce the same quota of bricks, but now you have to come up with your own straw. So you guys design the infrastructure and supply lines that I was providing for you. That ought to teach you a lesson about wanting to leave.

It was nothing short of a giant of increased hardship.

And it was all God's fault, right? The elders of Israel thought it was evil of God to do such a thing—and that certainly seemed to be the case. Even Moses saw it as evil in verses 22–23:

> Then Moses turned to the LORD and said, "O LORD, why have you done evil to this people? Why did you ever send me? For since I came to Pharaoh to speak in your name, he has done evil to this people, and you have not delivered your people at all."

If Gallup had taken a poll, about 99 percent of the Israelites would have agreed—yes, it was God's fault.

The entire nation was under increased hardship. Joshua and Caleb were young men at this time, and they weren't exempt from this fresh dump of extra pressure and pain. They faced that increased hardship along with everyone else, dealing with those excruciating days right along with their fathers, uncles, brothers, and cousins.

Here's the thing about increased hardship that seemingly comes from the hand of God:

- Increased hardship can lead you to bitterness, or …
- Increased hardship can lead you to brokenness

But it's only brokenness that can lead you to fruitfulness. Bitterness will never make you fruitful—it can only dry up your life and kill your hope for the future.

The Path of Brokenness

One of the finest books that I have read in a long time is Lon Solomon's book, *Brokenness*.

In 1992, Pastor Lon Solomon's career was on a speedy ascent. He was the senior pastor at McLean Bible Church, an influential and rapidly growing church in the suburbs of the nation's capital. In his weekly sermons he was funny, engaging, and self-effacing. He was successful, comfortable, respected by his peers, and reaching Washington's elite decision makers. His life could not have been better.

That's precisely when his world began to crumble.

He didn't see it at the time, but today Pastor Solomon knows that God was sending the blessing of brokenness to him. It came in the form of a beautiful daughter who for years would suffer through thousands of seizures and become severely impaired, physically and mentally. He and his family were thrust into days of emotional darkness. Pastor Solomon began to question his faith and feared he would fail his congregation.

In this touching and important book, he tells how God shattered him for the sole purpose of helping him reach his full potential as a servant of Christ. Today, his church is having a major impact on Washington, DC, with more than ten thousand worshippers attending services each weekend.[3]

Lon's book has great depth because he lives with a giant of increased hardship. He and his wife know what it is to be broken before God. What is brokenness? I like Lon's definition: "Brokenness is the process by which God dislodges our self-life and teaches us to rely upon him alone in every facet of our lives. Brokenness is the process whereby God crushes all our self-dependence and, in its place, substitutes an utter dependence on God and God alone in every area of our lives.… Through brokenness, God replaces our self-will with a surrender to the will and timing of God, tempering our human zeal with a deep waiting upon God."[4]

That's what the giant of increased hardship will do for you—and to you.

I'll never forget the first time I visited the garden of Gethsemane in Jerusalem. We all know that Jesus anguished alone in prayer there before He was taken before Pilate. The garden of Gethsemane sits on the side of a steep hill just a short walk from the Old City of Jerusalem. That steep hill is known as the Mount of Olives. In the days of Jesus, it was literally covered with olive trees. Today, there aren't as many trees as before, but they're still there in abundance.

Right next to the old church that sits at the foot of the Mount of Olives, I saw something that stopped me in my tracks. It was an old olive press. The workers would take their olives and put them into this large stone laver. A heavy stone wheel would circle the exposed olives and pulverize and crush them—and then the valuable oil would be carefully captured.

In the previous chapter I quoted John J. Murray's statement that "the Greek word for 'tribulation' comes from the verb 'to press.' The word is used to describe the crushing of grapes and olives, and the figure suggests the heavy pressures of outward trouble or inward anguish." Now let's tie that in with "Gethsemane."

The word *Gethsemane* means olive press.[5] It was in that garden of the oil press that Jesus was broken and crushed as he contemplated the cross that loomed immediately before Him.

Mark 14:32–34 describes the crushing and brokenness:

> And they went to a place called Gethsemane. And he said to his disciples, "Sit here while I pray." And he took with him Peter and James and John, and began to be greatly distressed and troubled. And he said to them, "My soul is very sorrowful, even to death. Remain here and watch."

Luke 22:44 describes the incredible anguish of His brokenness:

And being in an agony he prayed more earnestly; and his
sweat became like great drops of blood falling down to
the ground.

He experienced incomprehensible internal anguish before He ever
went to the cross. The Lord Jesus was crushed in that garden of the olive
press—and He was crushed for us. And then He went to the cross to die
in our place, giving His body and His blood to pay for our sin. Because we
have been called and redeemed by Him, there will be times when we will
encounter crushing and brokenness—as He did. It's the giant of increased
hardship.

Broken Dreams

Just last week I was talking with a man in his midthirties. Ten years ago
he married a beautiful woman who was as committed to Christ as he was.
But things have changed horrifically. And as a result, this man was telling
me that all of his Christian friends are telling him to leave—but he can't.
"There is a brake on my conscience, Steve. I can't leave. I'm not supposed
to leave. I'm staying for my kids. But I am absolutely at the end of my
rope. I'm exhausted and I'm weak and I wonder how long I can go on."

Here's a man in the olive press.

Here's a man in Gethsemane.

Here's a man facing the giant of increased hardship.

When he uttered those words to me, I said, "You sound just like the
apostle Paul." And then I opened my Bible to 2 Corinthians 1:8 (NASB):

For we do not want you to be unaware, brethren, of our
affliction which came to us in Asia, that we were burdened

excessively, beyond our strength, so that we despaired even
of life.

He read those words very slowly. Then he read them again, and he
said, "burdened excessively—beyond our strength." He paused for several
seconds, and thoughtfully said, "We despaired even of life."

He looked at me and said, "Steve, that's me. That's exactly how I feel.
I wish that I could die."

And I replied, "Can you believe that this is the apostle Paul writing? He
was absolutely broken at this point. He would have been utterly happy if
the Lord had said that he would be killed in the next sixty seconds. He was
so miserable that he would have welcomed death."

That's the giant of increased hardship.

And that's the olive press.

It is the place of complete crushing and utter brokenness. And Christ
is right there with you.

If you ask Him to use you, at some point you will find yourself in the
olive press. The olive press is the place of increased hardship. You've already
got hardship, but now something else comes into your life that you didn't
foresee, and it puts a burden on you that is so grievous you can hardly
breathe.

When the giant of increased hardship shows up, your life suddenly gets
worse. Much worse. Just like the men of Israel who now were responsible to
bring in tons of straw on a daily basis. Joshua and Caleb felt the full weight
of the increased hardship as young men—little did they know how God
was using it to prepare them for the great work that He had for them in
the years ahead.

The giant of increased hardship can show up in your life in a thousand
different ways.

Just ask Benaiah.

Mighty Man, Mighty Battle

Benaiah was one of David's mighty men, and a man David counted on throughout his life. He was the trusted captain of David's personal bodyguard (2 Sam. 23:23). When David was old and dying, Benaiah stood by his son Solomon and became chief of the entire army (1 Kings 2:35).

Benaiah himself had taken on an Egyptian giant and killed him with the giant's own weapon (2 Sam. 23:21). He was a man who was greatly used of God—so of course, he too had to fight the giant.

But what stands out with Benaiah is one of the most unusual stories ever recorded in the Old Testament. The entire story is told in just one brief sentence. But it is such a significant event that here we are, three thousand years later, looking into it.

The increased hardship came into Benaiah's life in a flash. It's very apparent that he never saw this life-threatening event coming. It came at him fast, a classic blindside. And immediately everything in his life became *worse*. Why?

Here's the one-sentence description of what happened to Benaiah from 2 Samuel 23:20 (NASB): "*He also went down and killed a lion in the middle of a pit on a snowy day.*"

Now stop and sink your teeth into that for a minute.

Increased hardship? Oh man. Can you imagine anything worse than killing a lion (not with a high-powered rifle from three hundred yards) in a pit (that's hand-to-paw combat) on a snowy day (it's tough to keep your footing on snow and ice)?

This was a life-threatening event for Benaiah.

I can read this account in my easy chair with a cup of coffee and think, *This is very interesting.* It was also very interesting to Benaiah, because he was facing the fetid breath and razor-sharp claws of a half-insane killer trapped in a pit the size of a broom closet.

May I point something out?

This really happened. This isn't a fable, or some comic book superhero in a Hollywood movie with special effects. This is recorded history. It happened just as surely as you getting out of bed this morning.

Fighting in a pit on a snowy day? That's what you call an intense aerobic workout. Years ago, the great preacher of New Zealand, Frank W. Boreham, did a sermon on Benaiah and the lion. Boreham made three classic observations about Benaiah:

- He met the *worst* of enemies (the lion)
- in the *worst* of places (a pit)
- under the *worst* of conditions (a snowy day).[6]

It doesn't get much *worse* than that!

And what did Benaiah do in that situation? Did he cry about his unfair circumstances or try to melt into the crowd at the edge of that pit? No, man of God that he was, Benaiah just rolled up his sleeves and took care of business. It's another example of a man who desired to be used by God facing the giants. And this giant of increased hardship is one of the toughest you will ever encounter.

It's one thing to face a lion. When David was a kid guarding his father's sheep, he took on a lion in the course of his shepherd duties. He may have been little more than a teenager at the time, but he didn't face that lion in a pit, and it wasn't on a snowy day.

Taking on a lion just in itself brings a certain measure of stress into a man's life—but in a pit—on a snowy day? That's increased hardship.

I wish that we had more details on this lion hunt, don't you? It raises all kinds of questions that the text doesn't answer. But we do know this: His very existence was threatened by this increased hardship.

But here's the good news. The text says that Benaiah killed the lion. The lion didn't kill Benaiah. When he found himself in a small pit with snow and perhaps ice under his feet, it was a very real possibility that the headlines would read "Lion Kills Benaiah."

But it didn't work out that way. God gave Benaiah a remarkable victory over the worst possible enemy in the worst possible place under the worst of conditions.

So here's a principle that you can count on:

Facing the giant of increased hardship means that deliverance is right around the corner.

Actually, that's not quite correct. I wish it was correct, but what I wish was true really doesn't enter into the equation. Allow me to restate that principle and then add another:

Facing the giant of increased hardship means that deliverance is right around the corner—maybe.

Or it could mean that:

Facing the giant of increased hardship means that deliverance is coming— but it may take awhile.

Here's the point: Whether deliverance is right around the corner or even if it will take awhile, it *is* coming. And it will come at the exact right time.

Will you be delivered? Absolutely. Joshua and Caleb were delivered and so was the apostle Paul. In 2 Corinthians 1:9–10 (NASB), he gives the report: "Indeed, we had the sentence of death within ourselves so that we would not trust in ourselves, but in God who raises the dead; who delivered us from so great a peril of death, and will deliver us...."

Can you count on deliverance from the giant of increased hardship? Absolutely. But it will come in God's perfect timing. Paul states this fact in Galatians 6:9 (NASB): "Let us not lose heart in doing good, for *in due time* we will reap if we do not grow weary." When deliverance is due, God will guarantee that it will show up.

So what is the purpose of the giant of increased hardship? Did you see it in 2 Corinthians 1:9–10? Paul said we have the sentence of death within ourselves so that we might trust not in ourselves, but in God who raises the dead.

Trust Me

This is all about learning to trust in the living God.

But we tend to trust in ourselves, don't we? So the Lord sends along the giant of increased hardship and turns up the heat in our lives. And we're not sure that we can take it. That's why we get broken. But it's all for a purpose that Thomas Watson describes so well:

> Water in the glass looks clear, but set it on the fire, and the scum boils up. In prosperity a man seems to be humble and thankful, the water looks clear; but set this man a little on the fire of affliction, and the scum boils up— much impatience and unbelief appear….
>
> As we sometimes hold a crooked rod over the fire to straighten it; so God holds us over the fire of affliction to make us more straight and upright.[7]

That's absolutely on target.

When we are broken because of increased hardship, we simply have to trust in the goodness of God. He knows precisely how long to keep me in the fire to straighten me out. He knows how long to set me over the fire to get rid of the hidden scum of my heart.

This stuff isn't easy. But it is very necessary.

Just this morning I was eating breakfast in a local restaurant and reading the sports page, when a guy came up and tapped me on the shoulder.

I hadn't seen him in probably seven or eight years. We talked for a few minutes and I asked him where he was these days. He told me he was the pastor of a new church in a particular town in another state. I know a guy who has pastored in that town for twenty-five years, so I asked him if he knew my friend. Immediately, the man dropped his head for a brief second. Something was obviously wrong. He looked at me and said, "Steve, it's just so sad. Just last week he took off with a woman in the church and left his family."

I've been in a state of shock over that all day.

But can I tell you something that I've been pondering as I've been writing for the last couple of hours? That's why God brings the giant of increased hardship into our lives. Increased hardship is God's way of turning up the heat to get rid of scum that's hidden down deep in our hearts.

I'll be honest with you. This hasn't been the greatest week for me. I have been in the fire. I never have difficulty sleeping—but I have this week. I have been facing circumstances that have hit me unexpectedly from four different angles, and the stress has been nearly overwhelming. But compared to a lot of people that I know, I'm in pretty good shape. And I'm grateful for that. But I'm still in the fire, and you know what? I *need* to be in the fire. It keeps me from getting cocky and arrogant. The fire keeps me desperately aware of my need for God's help.

I like sitting by a fire as well as anyone. There's nothing like a crackling fire in the fireplace on a cold December day. And telling stories around a campfire on a starry night isn't a bad way to invest a couple of hours. I like fire all right; I just don't like being *in* the fire.

Just lately, I've felt a little like one of those chickens that you see roasting over an open flame. And as I have been hanging over the fire a little bit this week, I've been saying some words that I normally don't say—in private. That tells me I've got some anger I need to deal with, because I don't *like* this. What I'm pointing out to you is that there is still quite a bit of scum in my heart that comes to the surface whenever I'm hanging over the fire.

How about you?

That scum that is hidden in my heart can not only get angry, but also if it is unchecked for any length of time, it can easily begin to rationalize sin. That's how solid men who have been used by God find themselves compromising their principles in private with some chick they shouldn't be with.

That's why I need the fire of affliction. There are just too many impurities in my heart and life. And if God doesn't boil them to the surface, they can do horrific damage to my life. Thank God for the fire.

Bitterness

If we're not careful, this giant of increased hardship can turn our hearts against the Lord. That's why we have to take caution with our thoughts and attitudes on a moment-to-moment basis.

When God brings the giant of increased hardship into our lives we have to consciously think rightly about God. If we're not careful when we are put over the fire, instead of the scum coming up out of our hearts, it can actually increase and lead to hardened bitterness. And that must be avoided at all costs. A heart full of bitterness toward God can lead one's mind to not only become unhealthy but untruthful. It's possible to become sick in the mind.

If you have seen Ben Stein's remarkable movie, *Expelled*, you have seen him interview some of the world premier atheists, men who sit at the top of the academic and atheistic world. But as you watch their statements and conclusions given in accurate context, you can only shake your head in amazement at their lack of mental health and sense of reality. It's really somewhat astonishing how such bitterness toward God can produce such obvious foolishness that a ten-year-old could pick apart.

Stein's movie is all about the academic world's insistence on the accuracy of Darwin's theory of evolution. Darwin's theory has become sacred scripture in the academic and scientific world. His book, *On the Origin of Species*, takes God completely out of the picture. According to modern science, the origin of the world was not God—it must be anything *but* God. That's why such a respected thinker (in the academic world) as atheist Richard Dawkins tells Ben Stein that life began on earth when aliens from another planet came to earth. It absolutely cannot be God! But the best he can do instead of God is aliens in a spaceship. It's absolute insanity—a shocking mental health deficit. And it always seems to start with a dislike and a bitterness toward God.

One popular Bible paraphrases Romans 1:19–23 (MSG) like this:

> But the basic reality of God is plain enough. Open your eyes and there it is! By taking a long and thoughtful look at what God has created, people have always been able to see what their eyes as such can't see: eternal power, for instance, and the mystery of his divine being. So nobody has a good excuse. What happened was this: People knew God perfectly well, but when they didn't treat him like God, refusing to worship him, they trivialized themselves into silliness and confusion so that there was neither sense nor direction left in their lives. They pretended to know it all, but were illiterate regarding life.

Silliness and confusion ... neither sense nor direction.

That paints a pretty accurate picture of today's academia, doesn't it? And bitterness, too—stemming from a steadfast refusal to trust God and

His unseen purposes. Did you know that Charles Darwin had only one academic degree? Do you know what he majored in at Cambridge? Darwin's degree from Cambridge was in theology. Not botany or biology—theology. Before Darwin sailed on the ship *The Beagle*, he actually said that he held to the inspiration of the Bible. Yet for years, a number of doubts had troubled his mind and his thinking.

The first doubt had to do with the whole issue of hell.[8] He secretly became angry and bitter at God. What right did God have to send anyone to hell? He could not believe that a good and gracious God would do such a thing. He wanted God to explain Himself further to him before he would trust Him when it came to eternal punishment. But God doesn't meet our demands to explain Himself.

God doesn't submit Himself to our cross-examinations. He tells us that He is good and righteous, and then asks us to trust Him. But Darwin couldn't do that. So he drifted into the scum of bitterness because of the increased hardship that God would put upon some people for eternity.

After he returned from his five-year voyage, he swore he would never go to sea again, and he never did. He lived on his estate in Down, England, with his wife, who was a committed Christian. But when their daughter, Annie, died at the age of ten, and then the following year his baby son died, the bitterness toward God began to rage anew.[9] Darwin had met the giant of increased hardship—and it was making him increasingly bitter toward God. As he worked as an amateur naturalist, he seethed in his heart toward a God who would cause such misery and suffering as he was experiencing. And instead of trusting—he continued to wallow in the scum of indicting God.

Do you see how the giant of increased suffering was moving him away from submission and brokenness to God? This is the temptation that we all face when it comes our way.

Spider Man

Now let's turn to the man who many believe is the greatest thinker in the history of America. His name is Jonathan Edwards and he was a pastor, a philosopher, and a president of Princeton University. Edwards loved the Lord his God with all his soul, all his strength, and all his might. In his teenage years, however, Edwards had done some struggling of his own with the existence, power, and goodness of God.[10] He wrestled in his mind with issues pertaining to the sovereignty of God, including the issue of hell, which seemed to him "a horrible doctrine."[11] The struggle nearly broke him.

Edwards was as fascinated with bugs, plants, and science as Darwin would be nearly a century later. But as he studied, he kept his heart open even as he struggled with deep questions. As a young man he did research on spiders that gained widespread admiration. He was mesmerized by spiders and their seeming ability to fly between trees because of their God-given filament. That filament not only enables them to travel, but also to craft webs that are engineering marvels. The more Edwards studied nature, the more he saw the hand of God. And he knew that he had been called for the rest of his life to declare the truth of this glorious God.[12]

So we have two men who deeply struggled over the same issues. One took the path of fruitfulness, but the other became bitter toward God. Bitterness began to slowly creep into every area of Darwin's existence. Toward the end of his life, Darwin wrote in his diary that he actually had lost his taste for literature and good music. He used to love the prose of Shakespeare, but as the years went by, Shakespeare made him literally sick to his stomach.[13] Beautiful music was no longer a joy to him.

Why? It was because of his increasing bitterness toward the God who had brought such incredible hardship to the world. If this was the same God who created beautiful scenery and gifted men to write pieces of literature and glorious music, then how could any of it be enjoyed? If this God was Creator and the very source of life, then how could he enjoy life itself? Darwin lost his very taste for life, and bitterness ruled his soul. It caused him to lose his mental health, in the sense that he couldn't enjoy the wonderful gifts of God that used to bring him such pleasure. The bitterness over increased hardship affected every area of his life. He bowed to bitterness instead of God, and in so doing, made the worst of all choices.

I began this chapter with the story of the great English architect A. W. N. Pugin. "In 1844 Pugin built a home for himself in Ramsgate, Kent, overlooking the sea. From the library of this rather severe house, called The Grange, Pugin did most of his work. Architecture, however, didn't take up his entire attention at The Grange; from the tower of the house Pugin would watch for ships aground off the Goodwin Sands. He would put out in his wrecker, *The Caroline*, to rescue the ships and cargo. The salvage money he gained from these rescues brought him a tidy supplement to his income from architecture."[14]

Just as Pugin would set out in his boat to rescue the cargo, so we too must make sure that we are putting forth every effort to rescue our hearts and minds from bitterness—bitterness that comes from the giant of increased hardship. And when we do so it will bring great profit to our souls and our daily existence.

The writings of Jonathan Edwards to this day point thousands to the greatness of the God who can be trusted, even when increased hardship comes our way. He is the God who uses adversity to train and prepare us for good works, not only in this life, but in eternity as well.

Edwards knew increased hardship throughout his life. But he saw the goodness of God even in the trials. Both Edwards and Darwin are no longer on the earth. They are in eternity. Edwards still holds to his view of God. And I would strongly suggest that Darwin no longer holds to his.

Increased hardship can lead you to one of two places: brokenness or bitterness.

Don't let bitterness grip your heart.

It's the straw that can break your heart—for eternity.

Chapter Six

Circling the Airport

"He writes in characters too grand
For our short sight to understand."
—*John Oxenham*

Nate Miller is a Brit who lives in Africa. Last June he was flying home from a business trip, looking forward to seeing his family. As the 737 started its descent, the aircraft took a couple of very sharp turns and then began to dive toward the runway. Passengers screamed as oxygen masks dropped. Slamming into the tarmac, the plane began a horrific slide across the end of the runway and through the outer barrier of the airport.

Nate looked up and all hell had broken loose.

Some people around him were bleeding and others were dead. He jumped out the emergency exit and immediately used his cell phone to call for help. The front of the aircraft was torn off the fuselage. As he ran around the front of the plane to see the damage, he saw that the plane had slid into a house.

It suddenly dawned on him that the half-destroyed house looked very familiar. It was his neighbor's house. He turned and looked across the street and there was his own house, looking just as it did before he left on his trip.

The trip didn't turn out exactly the way he thought it would.[1]

Joshua and Caleb could relate. Their trip wasn't turning out the way they had hoped either.

Post-Unbelief Analysis

Now let's see if we can get this straight.

Ten of the spies said, "We are not able to take on these giants. Let's go back." Joshua and Caleb stood against them and tried to convince the people that God would give a great victory.

So Joshua and Caleb are the good guys. The ten other yo-yos are the bad guys. Now watch what happens as described in Numbers 14:36–38:

> And the men whom Moses sent to spy out the land, who returned and made all the congregation grumble against him by bringing up a bad report about the land—the men who brought up a bad report of the land—died by plague before the LORD. Of those men who went to spy out the land, only Joshua the son of Nun and Caleb the son of Jephunneh remained alive.

So the ten bad guys die in a plague that the Lord sent upon them—which makes perfect sense to me. And what about Joshua and Caleb? Because of their faithfulness to the Lord, the plague doesn't touch them. So out of the original twelve spies, only these two guys are spared. That also makes sense to me.

But now, Joshua and Caleb are going to have to wait *forty years* before they go into the Promised Land.

Does that make any sense to you?

Because of the unbelief of the ten, Joshua and Caleb, along with Moses and Aaron, are going to have to wait and wander for forty years before God will allow them to cross over the Jordan River and actually go into the land and subdivide it.

But Joshua and Caleb did what was right! Why would they have to wait for forty years? That just doesn't add up ... does it? John Oxenham captures it all so well in a piece he titled "God's Handwriting":

> He writes in characters too grand
>> For our short sight to understand;
>> We catch but broken strokes, and try
>> To fathom all the mystery
>> Of withered hopes, of death, of life,
>> The endless war, the useless strife—
>> But there, with larger, clearer sight,
>> We shall see this—His way was right.[2]

God doesn't always make sense to us. The fact is, we're just not able to make out His handwriting at times. But that shouldn't be a surprise. He *told* us we wouldn't understand in Isaiah 55:8–9:

> For my thoughts are not your thoughts,
>> neither are your ways my ways, declares the LORD.
> For as the heavens are higher than the earth,
>> so are my ways higher than your ways
>> and my thoughts than your thoughts.

The handwriting of God expresses His thoughts. And sometimes His thoughts are more than we can fathom. It's like hooking up a little flashlight bulb to a bolt of lightning. We're overpowered! And we just don't get what He's up to. Why in the world would two guys who got it so right—who took the risk to stand against the crowd and do the right thing—get sentenced to forty years of wandering in a desolate desert with the faithless ones who had whined, complained, and jettisoned their faith at the first rumor of trouble?

In the short verse by John Oxenham, there are two very poignant words. Now I don't often use the word *poignant*. Poignant means to cause a sharp sense of sadness, pity, or regret. But when Oxenham speaks of "withered hopes," that is very poignant. Withered hopes bring great sadness into our lives.

Don't you think that Joshua and Caleb had to deal with "withered hopes" when they found out that they were going to have to wait for forty years to go into the land? You bet they did. That wasn't an easy pill to swallow.

They were about to take on *the giant of maintenance and monotony*.

What are we talking about here? We're talking about a long season of non-events. In other words, nothing is happening. It's not a time of high productivity—and for most men, it's a real drag. For Joshua and Caleb, it was a season that would drag on for decades.

Every man who desires to be used by God will at some point encounter this giant of maintenance and monotony. This is a giant that never works alone. When a man hits this stretch of life, he will find himself acquainted with:

- Disappointments and delays
- Timing and transitions
- Preparation and promotion

If you are asking God to "use me," at some point you will find yourself in this season of life. It probably won't last forty years, but it will last long enough to build muscle into your soul and prepare you for the work He has for you to do. There's just no getting around it.

In essence, it's a period of time when you're not very productive or fruitful. It's an interval of life that can be frustrating to the extreme, especially if you happen to be a classic Type A personality. If your personality could be characterized as "results oriented," you may find yourself restless and unhappy in the season of non-events. Feeling like you're stuck in neutral, you start to despair of ever making any forward progress.

In the season of non-events, you never make a first down. It's always, eternally, third-and-one. And you can seemingly never get that one yard you need to earn a new set of downs. Frustrating? Oh man … you think sometimes it will drive you off the edge. But like them or not, seasons like these are necessary for the growth and maturing of our inner man. And they are an integral part of God's plan for your life.

The simple fact is, God will work *in* you before He works *through* you.

And that's the purpose of the giant of maintenance and monotony.

Disappointment

Phillip Keller was a remarkable Christian writer whose books have touched the lives of millions. He is best known for his classic, *A Shepherd Looks At Psalm 23*. In that small volume, Keller sheds astonishing insight concerning shepherds and sheep that most city folk would never have a clue about.

As a young man, however, Keller had no interest in sheep. His great love was cattle and his hope and dream was to own a cattle ranch:

> As a lad I had grown up with cattle. On our land in East Africa, my father had bred the finest of the breeds adapted to the tropics. His cattle were a special joy to him; the splendid bulls that sired our calves, the sturdy oxen that hauled

our wagons and worked our fields, the handsome cows that produced our milk were a marvel to the Africans.

When I came to North America to complete my university training in animal husbandry, cattle still played an important role in my career. I worked on various ranches and longed for the day when I would purchase my own "spread" and establish my own herd.

By my mid-twenties I had been made manager of one of the most beautiful ranches in the interior cattle country of British Columbia.... It was shortly after this that I found a piece of neglected ranch property at the southern tip of Vancouver Island. Because it was so abused the place did not attract much interest, but I could see its potential. It was an estate sale, so cash had to be paid for the property.

The net result was that I had insufficient funds left to purchase cattle, so I was obliged to start out with sheep.[3]

When Keller writes that sentence, you should understand that it was a profound disappointment in his life. *Sheep?* For years and years, since boyhood, he had wanted to be a cattle rancher. He had spent hundreds of hours with cattle, studied for a number of years at the University of Toronto to earn his degree in animal husbandry, and scrimped and saved every spare dime when he was managing a large cattle ranch. He had put years and years of work and study into his dream, and then when the day came that he was finally able to buy his own ranch, he didn't have the money to buy cattle. All he could afford were sheep. It was a great disappointment and somewhat of an embarrassment to young Keller.

Keller's parents were missionaries to East Africa. And even though he had been raised by Christian parents, it took him years to truly embrace

Christ as his Lord and Savior. But once he did, it became his passion to be used by God. And it was his great disappointment that enabled him to be used beyond his wildest dreams.

As a result of spending those early years with the sheep, Keller learned lessons and applications that would be read by over *two million people.* Keller never wrote a book about cattle, but he did write a book about sheep. And to this day, it is a classic that thrills every reader with insights and truths from God's Word that Keller learned every day in raising those sheep. And as it happened, he learned those valuable insights in the midst of great disappointment and delay.

Life is full of disappointments. But God uses disappointments to shape us, teach us, and eventually use us. He also uses such setbacks to save us from the foolishness of our own plans. That often means that we encounter significant and unwanted delays.

Delays

Joshua and Caleb hold the world record for delays.

They had to wait for forty years before they could enter into the Promised Land and begin the work that God had called them to do.

It's natural for us to want the delays in our lives to be as brief as possible. For some reason ("My ways are not your ways"), God operates on a different approach to scheduling.

John Newton was not only the writer of great hymns such as "Amazing Grace," but a gifted and much-respected pastor. Newton had been the captain of a slave ship when the Lord reached down and changed his heart. He began to grow in his faith and develop a hunger for the Word. After his conversion, he took two more voyages to Africa. But the night before his third voyage, Newton became violently ill. John Newton was one of those men who never got sick—he had the constitution of a draft horse. But this sudden stroke was so severe that he couldn't get out of bed. The ship was forced to sail with another captain due to Newton's extreme condition. Within hours of the ship's departure, Newton got up out of his bed in the peak of health.

The sickness was a divine delay that ended one chapter of Newton's life and began another. In a matter of hours, his sailing days were over. He became Surveyor of the Tides for the port of Liverpool, and held that position for the next five years.

But all the while, something was stirring in Newton's heart. He believed that the Lord was calling him to become a pastor, and began a diligent study of the Scriptures. He taught himself Hebrew and Greek so that he could study the Bible in the original languages, and began to teach a small gathering of Christians—who gave him tremendous feedback.

He finally took the step of seeking ordination to preach. But in spite of his obvious giftedness and diligence, time and again he was denied. The bishop wouldn't even let him be considered. It was one delay after another, and Newton wasn't getting any younger. It was all the more frustrating for Newton because he felt like he'd already wasted his younger years. But now, in his quest to serve God as a pastor, he experienced one setback after another, disappointment after disappointment, delay and delay. And then after five agonizingly slow years, he was ordained and given a pastorate in Olney.

It wasn't a forty-year delay, but five years was long enough.

But Newton learned that it was a necessary delay. He penned the following insights on disappointments and delays in a personal letter dated August 17, 1767:

> It is indeed natural to us to wish and to plan, and it is
> merciful in the Lord to disappoint our plans, and to cross
> our wishes. For we cannot be safe, much less happy, but
> in proportion as we are weaned from our own wills, and

made simply desirous of being directed by His guidance. This truth (when we are enlightened by His Word) is sufficiently familiar to the judgment; but we seldom learn to reduce it to practice, without being trained awhile in the school of disappointment. The schemes we form look so plausible and convenient, that when they are broken, we are ready to say, What a pity! We try again, and with no better success; we are grieved, and perhaps angry, and plan out another, and so on; at length, in a course of time, experience and observation begin to convince us, that we are not more able than we are worthy to choose aright for ourselves. Then the Lord's invitation to cast our cares upon Him, and His promise to take care of us, appear valuable; and when *we* have done planning, *His* plan in our favour gradually opens, and He does more and better for us than we either ask or think.

I can hardly recollect a single plan of mine, of which I have not since seen reason to be satisfied, that had it taken place in season and circumstance just as I proposed, it would, humanly speaking, have proved my ruin; or at least it would have deprived me of the greater good the Lord had designed for me. We judge of things by their present appearances, but the Lord sees them in their consequences, if we could do so likewise we should be perfectly of His mind; but as we cannot, it is an unspeakable mercy that He will manage for us, whether we are pleased with His management or not; and it is spoken of as one of His heaviest judgments, when He gives any person or people up to the way of their own hearts, and to walk after their own counsels.[4]

Newton spoke of "the school of disappointment." Have you ever done any course work in that school? Newton knew it well because of the five-year delay. Painful delays teach us valuable lessons in "the school of disappointment." But none of us would ever sign up for the classes—so God signs us up and puts us in the school that we try so diligently to avoid. Disappointments and delays can literally make us sick at heart. Proverbs 13:12 (NASB) diagnoses it well:

> Hope deferred makes the heart sick,
> But desire fulfilled is a tree of life.

Timing

Delays and disappointments make us sick at heart because we're aware of time slipping away from us. We have a sense that if something doesn't happen right now, it won't ever happen, and the opportunity will be lost forever.

Joshua and Caleb didn't experience a plane crash in their front yard, they experienced something quite different. They didn't crash as they came into the airport. They just circled the airport—for forty years.

Can you imagine what these two men faced every morning? They knew they had been put on hold for forty years. I can imagine them checking off the calendar and counting how many days were left before another year would go by. But then they still had many years ahead of them for their desire to be fulfilled.

Sometimes God's timing makes absolutely no sense to us. We can't see any good reason for it!

When Phillip Keller bought his ranch, there was something he had to do before he purchased any sheep. He had to find a sheep dog. In his remarkable book *Lessons from a Sheep Dog*, he tells the story of finding a two-year-old sheep dog who had been severely abused. Keller couldn't afford a sheep dog that had been fully trained, so he took a chance on a dog that was probably so damaged that she would never learn to be obedient. But Keller had no choice. So he took the little abused border collie home, and she snapped at him all the way. He couldn't get close to her and she wouldn't respond.

Although the dog's new surroundings were clean and she was given a first-rate kennel, she became even more difficult and withdrawn. Provided with good food, clean water, and a good bed, she became more and more depressed. At one point, Keller actually thought she was going to die.

Finally after weeks of watching the little dog deteriorate, Keller made a daring move. He opened the gate of the kennel and set her free. She ran like a rocket into the forest, and Keller wondered if he would ever see Lass again. He would set food and water out for her every day. But Lass was gone.

The food and water were gone each morning—but he wasn't sure it was Lass. It might have been some other animal who was feasting on Lass's dinner.

I won't tell the whole story here, but in a remarkable turn of events, little Lass, the abused border collie, one day came home. And from then on, Keller began to train this little dog to inherit her destiny. She was bred to herd sheep, but she had to obey the commands of her master. Extremely intelligent, she quickly learned the commands and signals:

Come—Lie down—Sit—Fetch them—Stay—To the left—To the right.

There was one command that was more difficult for Lass than any of the others. Keller writes,

> Strange as it may seem, the most difficult command for
> her to comply with was *Stay*. Sometimes it meant that she
> would have to hold a bunch of lambs in the corner of a
> field or guard a gate or keep watch over some unruly rams

while I was doing another job. It was very trying for her to have me disappear from view. She was eager to be where the action was.[5]

Now that doesn't describe us? We want to be where the action is—we don't want to be delayed or deterred in any way. And when we are delayed, we get extremely disappointed, and we begin to question our Master. There is no harder command than *stay*.

Stay is all about God's timing.

The Master knows things we know nothing about—a perspective and purpose beyond our comprehension. From where we sit, we can't see what He's up to. But when He says "Stay," even if it's for forty years, we had better stay. Never fight or buck the timing of God.

When God tells us to stay, it's often a command that runs absolutely against the grain of our ambitions and plans. We want to be where the action is! We don't want to be stalled out in a season of non-events, where nothing seems to be happening, we're not achieving our goals, and we don't seem to be making anything of our lives.

These are times when we're not very motivated or excited about life. On the contrary, life begins to feel dull, routine, and colorless, and we have to fight off a sense of boredom or futility. With no big events to look forward to, we feel like we're simply maintaining.

So we find ourselves wanting to bolt—wanting to leave—wanting to make things happen. Instead of staying, we want to bust out of the kennel.

If that's where you are right now, allow me to offer some serious counsel. Be very careful, my friend. Bolting is not the answer, no matter how bored and frustrated you may feel at the moment.

For you see, it's in the season of non-events that we learn to be faithful. And nothing is more valued by the Master. What is required of a steward is that he be found faithful—not bolting, not running, not fleeing—but faithful.

Learning to be faithful where God has placed you is the equivalent of a border collie *staying*.

So don't bolt.

Don't run.

Stay.

When the timing is right in God's plan, He will throw open the door of your kennel, and you will have no doubt at all. (God also knows how to build a fire under His servants and get them moving!) The opportunity will finally arrive, and you won't be able to miss it. But when that door finally does open, you may find yourself entering yet another phase of your season of non-events.

It's called a transition.

Transitions

Over the years, I've read a ton of books on leadership. One of the very best is *The Making of a Leader*, written by J. Robert Clinton. When I was thirty-nine years old and in the sixth year of fighting the giant of maintenance and monotony, I was just about at the end of my rope. I wanted to be used by God—but I was six years into delay and disappointment. Nothing was working. I wasn't productive in my ministry. My church wasn't growing. More were leaving than coming in—and I'm a results-oriented guy. It was killing me. I felt like my life was wasting away. All I was doing was maintaining, and the monotony and boredom were excruciating for me. On top of all that, the church leaders I'd been working with began to turn on me. Let's just say that things weren't looking up.

And one day, in a little bookstore hidden away in a run-down shopping center, I found Clinton's book—and devoured it in two days. And something happened to me as I read and marked the pages. I found hope.

The copy on the back cover of that book explains why I found hope: "In *The Making of A Leader*, Dr. Robert Clinton identifies the patterns God uses to develop a leader. By studying the lives of hundreds of historical, biblical, and contemporary leaders, Dr. Clinton has determined the six stages of leadership development, and he establishes checkpoints to clarify where you are in the process."[6]

It was one of those rare times in life when the Lord gives you a bit of perspective, and you catch a quick glimpse—a flash of insight—of where you've been, where you are, and where you're going. I was given hope as I read Clinton's study of biblical leaders because he demonstrated that there is a six-phase process that God uses to develop His leaders. And as you move from one phase to the next, you will find yourself *in transition.*

Transition! That's exactly where I was in life, but I hadn't been able to see it. What a surge of hope I felt in that moment! And nineteen years later, as I look back, I can tell you that Clinton was dead on.

When I read his book, I was in what I would call "the season of non-events." Clinton would refer to it as two phases: life maturing and ministry maturing, which one usually experiences simultaneously.

The six phases are:

1. Sovereign Foundations
2. Inner-life Growth
3. Ministry Maturing
4. Life Maturing
5. Convergence
6. Afterglow

As I read his book, it became clear to me that God was about to transition me from phases 3 and 4 into phase 5, which is *convergence*—a stage of life where you become fruitful and productive. After years of being trained in the season of non-events, after nearly drowning in wave after wave of disappointment and delay, God transitions a man who has been teachable into convergence.

When you get into convergence, you will find a place of ministry and effectiveness where your strengths and gifts are maximized and your weaknesses are covered. In Clinton's own words, "[In convergence], the leader uses the best he has to offer and is freed from ministry for which he is not gifted or suited."[7]

Now here's the point. If you identify with finding yourself fighting maintenance and monotony and you've been there quite awhile, you should be encouraged. If you have been teachable and responsive to the Lord, if you are seeking Him by knowing His Word and applying it to your life, before long you will see Him bring about a transition in your life.

I want you to catch this: *You don't have to make the transition happen.* That's God's work. You don't have to scheme and force events and wear out your brain trying to figure everything out. What do you do, then? You stay faithful as best you can to your current assignment from the Lord, and make sure you obey the command to stay.

Yes, you may find yourself bored at times. But you can also be hopeful! God is up to something, and He's getting you ready for a slot that will maximize your gifts and strengths. But remember, only God can bring about the transition. You can't manipulate your way to the place of His appointment.

As I read Clinton's book, it seemed to me that I was due for a transition. And I was right. Within six months I found myself very strongly encouraged to leave my ministry position.

Like, immediately.

No, that wasn't exactly the transition I was expecting. But it was the one that God used to open the kennel door.

If you will be faithful and stay, you will learn a number of important lessons. And those lessons will come through isolation, crisis, and conflict.[8]

But in those difficult class sessions of maintenance and monotony, you will learn what you are good at and what you are not gifted to do. You will learn your real strengths and your weaknesses. Those are valuable insights that prepare you for the unique work God has for you to do. But you don't learn those things overnight.

When the lessons have been well and truly learned (and only God is judge of that), it will be time for the gate to open, swinging you into a transition that will take you to yet another chapter in your life.

Be aware that God can use a conflict or an economic hardship to provide the transition. In Robert Clinton's own case, he was shown the door and asked to clean out his desk after years of service to a missions organization. It wasn't pleasant and it wasn't pretty. It was more like a kick in the gut. But it's what God used to get Clinton to his own personal place of convergence.

I was reading the other day about George Washington (it's my hobby, remember?). Not only was he a great military leader and our first president, but first and foremost he was a Virginia planter. Not a farmer, but a planter. And in Virginia back in those days, a gentleman planter had just one crop—tobacco. But suddenly, Washington found himself, along with many other Virginia planters, in a credit crunch. Most of the other planters just kept going with what they had always done, and that was to keep planting tobacco. Even though they were going deeper and deeper into debt, they kept planting and planting as they had always done. It was simply what a gentleman farmer did; never mind the fact that it wasn't working anymore.

Washington could read the bottom line and knew he was in some financial trouble. So he took the financial crisis as an indicator that he needed to make a transition. And what he did astonished his friends and neighbors. He decided to stop growing tobacco at Mount Vernon.[9] Washington was land rich and cash poor, so he planted wheat, buckwheat, corn, flax, and alfalfa—and immediately began to turn a profit. Seeing that this new course of action was bringing results, he stuck with it.

Richard Brookhiser has observed that "successful businessmen often change their business in midcareer. In the early nineteenth century, John Jacob Astor, America's first millionaire, switched from fur trading to New York City real estate; in midcentury, Cornelius Vanderbilt moved from shipping, which had given him the title Commodore, to railroads. Washington's switch was tougher, because it risked his prestige. By abandoning the cultivation of tobacco, he stepped outside the tobacco culture, surrendering his status as a planter, crop master, and lord of the soil, and becoming instead a farmer—a rich farmer, to be sure, though the term had, to older Virginian ears, a humbler sound."[10]

It may have given a humbler title, but it kept him out of bankruptcy. And many of the old established Virginian planters drove their way right into it, while Washington was putting money in the bank.

Sometimes economic crisis will bring the transition. A transition can come in your employment because of a conflict over the direction of the company. A transition can come in a hundred different ways.

But here's the million-dollar question: *How do you know when it's time to transition?* How do you know when it's time to shift gears from "stay" to "running out of the gate"?

In the season of maintenance and monotony, God is commanding you to *stay*. But when He's ready to give you a new command, it will come through loud and clear. You might get fired. Like George Washington, you may look at the bottom line of your business and say there's no way in the world I can keep doing this. Someone has said that insanity is doing the same thing over and over, and thinking that you will get a different result.

If it isn't clear to you that God is throwing the gate open, then stay.

If it seems that the gate has opened slightly, but you're not sure if that's a fact or just your imagination, then allow me to make a suggestion:

Seek godly counsel.

You shouldn't try to figure this out by yourself. Proverbs 11:14 indicates that "in an abundance of counselors there is safety."

I'll be honest with you, when I was asked point-blank to leave my ministry position, I was shocked and offended. It came with an early morning phone call that changed everything. In fifteen minutes I was out of a job. In hindsight, those leaders were simply acknowledging the facts. It was over (and had been over), and I needed to move on. (By the way, several years later I had a wonderful time of reconciliation with the key leader, and we both shook our heads at how God worked everything out.) But on that morning I couldn't see that. All I could see was red. I was angry.

When I got off the phone that morning, Mary had heard one side of the conversation, but as I filled her in on the details, I started to really get angry. And then I began to think about how I might mount a defense that would enable me to stay. As I began to verbally process my anger and strategy to Mary, she said to me, "Steve, do you think the Lord wants you to be here long term?"

I immediately replied, "No."

And then she asked, "Then why would you fight this?"

My reply was brief. "Because I'm an idiot."

That's literally what I said.

She then went on and said, "For the last three years, all of your closest friends have said that you should be doing conference ministry and writing full time. That would be the best use of your gifts. It would enable you to focus on what God has gifted you to do. Why don't we take this as God's way of launching you into that new ministry?"

I knew she was right. Men whom I greatly respected had been given me that feedback for several years. But it always seemed like something that might happen "sometime in the future." But now that future had suddenly arrived, and there could be no doubt. As soon as Mary made that statement, my anger was extinguished. I knew that God was moving me out. Actually, He was kicking me out. But I didn't want to go because I was afraid. I couldn't see any way that we could make it financially.

Usually when I would do an outside speaking engagement, I was fortunate enough to receive three or four requests to come and speak at churches or conferences. And I always said no because I had the responsibility of pastoring a church. Most often, the requests were for dates a year or so away.

So when Mary said to me, "Why don't we take this as God's way of moving you into full-time conferences and writing?" all I could see was fear.

"Mary, here's the problem. I've been turning down all kinds of invitations. But if I were to start saying yes today, it would be at least a year before I would begin doing those conferences and realizing any income. How in the world would we make it?"

Good woman that she is, Mary replied, "Steve, the Lord will take care of that. He will make a way."

"Yeah, I know—but how are we going to make it?"

Once again, that's literally what I said.

You see, I was suddenly in a major transition. I figured it would come one day, but not *that* day.

William Bridges has observed that transitions break up into three stages:

- Endings
- The Neutral Zone
- The New Beginning[11]

In my case, the giant of maintenance and monotony died so suddenly it stunned me. Just that quickly, I was no longer maintaining, and I was no longer bored. I was just scared spitless.

With the realization of that "ending" in my life, however, I immediately found myself in "the neutral zone." If indeed I was supposed to go into conference ministry and it could be a year before we experienced any income, how in the world would we make ends meet? How would I make my mortgage payment and feed my two kids? (I actually had three kids but at that moment I was so stressed out I couldn't exactly remember.)

This transition had slammed me head-on into a semi-truck. What would happen? How would we survive?

After that very eventful phone call at 7:30 a.m., life had to go on. Mary had to leave to run some errands and I was left by myself to figure out the rest of my life.

I will tell you this—I was so scared I could hardly swallow. All I could see was the next twelve months of no income.

So what did I do?

I took a two-hour walk through every street in our neighborhood and I literally "cried out" to God. In Psalm 57:2–3 (NASB), David says,

> I will cry to God Most High,
>> To God who accomplishes all things for me.
> He will send from heaven and save me.

Crying out to God is a prayer of absolute desperation. It's not a calm, easygoing kind of prayer like "Bless this food to the nourishment of our bodies." To be "desperate" (according to my dictionary software) is to be overwhelmed with urgency and anxiety, to the point of losing hope. And that definition fit me to a T, as I suddenly found myself forty-five minutes into a major life transition.

Now who is this God I was crying out to? He is the God who accomplishes all things for me. One of the old Puritans rendered that verse, "To God who is the transactor of all my affairs."

That's the God I serve. He is all powerful—and I was all freaked-out.

So in desperation, for two hours I walked the sidewalk of every street in our subdivision, crying out for Him to make a way. Because I could see no possible way that we could get through this.

I came back to the house just as Mary was pulling into the driveway. We both went into the house and within a couple of minutes the phone rang.

Two or three years before, Mary had been in an automobile accident that was the other guy's fault. She had to have some ongoing medical treatment and the insurance company refused to pay her medical bills until we signed a waiver releasing them of any further responsibility. Well, the doctor told us that she was going to be in treatment for months to come, so of course we didn't sign it. The insurance company refused to pay and the bills were stacking up. Finally I went to a Christian attorney that had been recommended to us. He assured us that he would represent us, but that we shouldn't expect any kind of quick resolution. He was right. It dragged on a year, and then another year.

And when the phone rang that morning, he was on the other end. He wanted me to know that he had a settlement. And by noon the next day he handed me a check for what amounted to nearly half of my annual salary.

I had been wondering how we were going to make it. But God, who accomplishes all things for me, the God who is the transactor of all my affairs, He had it worked out long before I had ever cried out to Him.

Earlier that morning, when I had been thrown into an "ending," I had no clue how we would get through the twelve-month "neutral zone." Little did I know that by *the next afternoon* I would have more money in my checking account than I had ever had in my entire life.

I was without a job and income. I had just come through maintenance and monotony. And I had close to six months' income in the bank for the first time in my life.

I felt like the children of Israel after they plundered the Egyptians of their silver and gold, just before they headed out to the Red Sea (Ex. 12:35–36).

Go figure.

Are you facing the giant of maintenance and monotony? If you are, you should be encouraged. That season of non-events is the period of life when God does the deep and tough work in the heart of a man He intends to use. And when He has completed that phase of His work, when you find yourself heartily sick of all the disappointment and delays, He will sovereignly work to put you in a place of maximum effectiveness.

What He has for you to do probably won't look like what He has for me to do. We are different in our gifts and He has designed us that way on purpose. We all have a work to do and no work is insignificant. So even though our individual gifts, talents, calling, and experience may be different, the process of preparation is the same. There are no shortcuts. I have yet to see a man used by God who did not taste of "the season of non-events."

It may be a long season in your life, but it is a temporary season.

On that bright, joyous morning after crossing the Red Sea, Joshua and Caleb were on their way to the Promised Land with a lift in their feet and a song in their hearts. As God had promised, He was bringing them to a land with houses they hadn't built, crops they hadn't planted, vineyards they hadn't tended, and cisterns they'd never had to dig. But because of the rank unbelief of the ten spies, all of that came to an end. For the next forty years they would be cooling their heels in the neutral zone.

But when the forty years came to an end, it was time for a new beginning.

I think they would tell us that it was worth the wait, and that they had become better men because of the disappointments and delays.

Even forty years is temporary when God is at work in your life. You won't be there permanently, as long as you are teachable and obedient. It's the preparation that is necessary for the promotion.

And don't worry about missing it. He's in charge of the transitions of your life, and He will get you where He wants you to be.

You can count on that—it's in the Word of God.

> The mind of man plans his way,
>   But the LORD directs his steps. (Prov. 16:9 NASB)

Chapter Seven

High Wire Promotion

"In God's world there is no substitute for full obedience."
—*James Montgomery Boice*

After forty years of waiting, things began to happen—fast.

Moses died and Joshua was named the new leader of Israel.

And Caleb? Well, he got mad, picked up his toys, and went home. He had wanted to be the leader himself, and it wasn't fair that Joshua got picked instead of him.

In case you're not familiar with the story, it didn't happen that way. But it's interesting that in so many churches and ministries, it *does* happen that way. Somebody gets mad because they didn't get the promotion.

And what does that prove? That they should never have gotten the promotion! Wanting to be in the spotlight or to have control is not how you qualify for leadership in the kingdom of God. Those kinds of attitudes are symptomatic of someone who is not ready for leadership. And if they somehow get into leadership, they will fail, because they don't have the maturity or obedience to do what God directs them to do.

It was an astonishing and brazen act when Palestinian terrorists took eleven Israeli athletes hostage at the 1972 Munich Olympic Games.

In response to that outrage, a team of elite German sharpshooters was brought in to take out the terrorists. Each of the sharpshooters had been promoted above his peers because of his superior skill. And as the situation unfolded, each of the sharpshooters had a terrorist in his sights. Yet when the command to "fire" was given, two of the snipers couldn't bring themselves to pull the trigger. As a result, every hostage was murdered within seconds.[1]

Yes, they were part of an elite team and had been promoted over their peers. They must have had a real sense of pride in their accomplishment. But in the moment of truth, two of them failed—and innocent lives were snuffed out as a result.

Because of their superior training and skill these sharpshooters had climbed the ladder of promotion. But in the critical moment, they fell from their elite position. They simply couldn't handle the responsibilities of the promotion. It was a tragic example of the Peter Principle at work.

Back in the seventies, Lawrence J. Peter wrote a book titled *The Peter Principle*. It was a smash hit. Peter observed that in a hierarchy every employee tends to rise to their level of incompetence. Two snipers could not pull the trigger because they couldn't handle the responsibilities of their promotion. Undoubtedly, they wanted the promotion and the adulation that came with it. But when the rubber met the road, they just simply couldn't cut it. And hostages died that day because of their incompetence.

Forty-Year Anniversary

Now let's get up to speed on where we are in the journey of Joshua and Caleb.

Forty years to the day after the ten spies had refused to fight the giants, Joshua was promoted and given the command to "move out." The waiting was over. Maintenance and monotony had run its course.

Phillip Keller writes: "The forty dreadful years in the desert had ground on remorselessly. The wilderness wastes took a steady toll on the Israelis.

Year after year the corpses of mature men and women were buried in the burning sands of the Arabian hinterland. It was a time of terrible attrition for those who left Egypt in high hopes only to perish in the wilderness because of their perverseness....

"It would be a tremendous turnaround for Israel. Instead of tramping dejectedly in circles of dusty old trails of desperation in the desert, now they would begin to move into new territory. Instead of blowing sand, burning rocks and scrub thorn, they would cross Jordan into fields of grain and groves of fruit. Instead of animal dung for fuel there would be forests of trees to cut for firewood. Instead of flimsy tents they would take over sturdy homes in strong cities with ample accommodation for their families."[2]

When the ten spies had failed to trust God, they had been killed in a plague. And the sentence for the rest of the unbelieving nation was that every adult over twenty would die in the next forty years—and therefore not go into the incredible land of God's provision. Only Joshua and Caleb were spared (Num. 14:30). And now it was time to take a new generation of Israelis into the land that had been promised so many years before.

The leadership of Israel had been transferred from Moses to Joshua. And it was time to get to work.

> After the death of Moses the servant of the LORD, the LORD said to Joshua the son of Nun, Moses' assistant, "Moses my servant is dead. Now therefore arise, go over this Jordan, you and all this people, into the land that I am giving to them, to the people of Israel. Every place that the sole of your foot will tread upon I have given to you, just as I promised to Moses. From the wilderness and this Lebanon as far as the great river, the river Euphrates, all the land of the Hittites to the Great Sea toward the going down of the sun shall be your territory. No man shall be

able to stand before you all the days of your life. Just as I
was with Moses, so I will be with you. I will not leave you
or forsake you. Be strong and courageous, for you shall
cause this people to inherit the land that I swore to their
fathers to give them. Only be strong and very courageous,
being careful to do according to all the law that Moses my
servant commanded you. Do not turn from it to the right
hand or to the left, that you may have good success [*act
wisely*] wherever you go. This Book of the Law shall not
depart from your mouth, but you shall meditate on it day
and night, so that you may be careful to do according to
all that is written in it. For then you will make your way
prosperous, and then you will have good success. Have I
not commanded you? Be strong and courageous. Do not
be frightened, and do not be dismayed, for the LORD your
God is with you wherever you go. (Josh. 1:1–9)

Finally, after forty years of waiting at a red light, the light turned green. The
task before them was enormous, and to top it off, Moses, who had led them
for forty years, was dead. And the leadership baton was handed to Joshua.

Proven, Then Promoted

The death of Moses was a huge turning point in the life of Joshua. How
would you like to be the leader that followed *Moses?* Admittedly, those were
some pretty big sandals to fill. Joshua had to replace a seemingly irreplaceable leader.

But the truth is, every leader is replaceable. Every leader is unique, but
no leader is irreplaceable. As someone has noted, there is one Lord, but

many servants. Moses was a servant of the living God who had been given a significant leadership position. But every man has his time and then is removed.

God had picked Joshua to step in as starting quarterback upon the death of Moses. It was a big promotion with an unbelievably rigorous assignment attached to it. He was to take the people into the land to fight and conquer all of the *-ites* (including the giants). He was then to oversee the distribution of the newly conquered land to each of the twelve tribes. And then he was responsible to lead the people into reaffirming their covenant with the Lord.[3]

Joshua was ready for the task. He had been a trusted lieutenant of Moses (Ex. 24:13; 33:11) and had proven his mettle in battle (Ex. 17:8–16). And along with courageous Caleb, he had shown his muster and faith by his willingness to take on the giants (Num. 14:6).

He was seasoned, he was tested, and then he was promoted. And when he got the Canaanites in his sights, he had no hesitation in pulling the trigger.

Yes, it was a lofty promotion to become the soldier-general of Israel as they went into battle after battle to take the land. But we should note something important about Joshua at this point.

Although he had been promoted, he hadn't politicked to get the job. He wasn't pursuing the top spot. He didn't brownnose the right people in order to increase his chances of making it to the top. He didn't pad his résumé, and he didn't undercut any potential rivals. Joshua didn't play any of the games that so many men play in order to make their way to the top.

It was a huge promotion, but he didn't seek it. He didn't scheme, he didn't maneuver, and he didn't schmooze. He never announced his intention to run for the position, and he didn't show up at any primaries. He was simply faithful in what God had given him to do. And at the appointed time, he was chosen by the Lord for the top slot (Num. 27:15–23).

And what about Caleb, the other guy who had bided his time for forty years in the desert? Did he get mad, pick up his bat, and go home? No, because he didn't have to be the top dog; that's why there is no report of a conflict or a problem. That's because Caleb was a mature man.

Many leaders in Christian churches, however, are not mature. Some of them aren't even true believers. There was a leader who caused some serious chaos in one of the New Testament churches. You can read it for yourself in the little New Testament letter called 3 John. The apostle John writes to the church, and addresses the problems that one man called Diotrephes is causing. John promises to handle Diotrephes when he visits them. But he diagnoses the root problem that controls every action and behavior that comes out of Diotrephes by saying Diotrephes "loves to be first among them" (3 John 1:9 NASB).

That's why this guy wanted to be in charge and loved the limelight. And because he loved to be first, he had to control everyone and everything around him. He wouldn't submit to the authority of the apostle John, who had been handpicked by the Lord Jesus Himself.

Neither Joshua nor Caleb loved to be first, had to be in charge, or angled to get into the limelight. That's why they got along so well for all of those years. They weren't rivals—they were friends. And when Joshua got the nod for the big-time promotion, Caleb was thrilled for him.

There is a lesson here, and we need to hear it: There is great wisdom in not promoting yourself. Let the Lord promote you (Ps. 75), and if a promotion comes, then you know that He was the one who did the promoting.

Yes, I understand that you want to do well in your career and provide for your family. Of course you do. You want to make a good living and advance in your work. Is there anything wrong with that?

It really all comes down to ambition—and what kind of ambition you possess. The New Testament speaks about two kinds of ambition: I call them authentic ambition and arsenic ambition. Scripture looks favorably on one, but the other is a demonic counterfeit.

Authentic Ambition

The apostle Paul mentions the good kind of ambition in 2 Corinthians 5:9 (NASB), where he says, "Therefore we also have as our ambition … to be pleasing to Him."

Notice the root of this ambition: It is to please the Lord. That's the motive of the man who wants to be used by God. No matter what he attempts, no matter what he puts his hand to, he wants to please the Lord. In this context, Paul is talking about the fact that he would rather just go ahead and go on to heaven. If he had his "druthers" between staying on earth or leaving his body behind and catching a direct flight to heaven, he would definitely choose making the trip and being with Jesus.

But bottom line, Paul wanted to please the Lord.

The idea of this word *please* is "to devote oneself zealously to a cause."[4] On top of all his other ambitions or desires, that was Job One for Paul—his strong desire and root motivation. He wanted to please the Lord and bring glory to God. In other words, he wanted to be used by God in whatever way might bring the most honor to God's name. (And, he had an ace in the hole. He knew he had heaven ahead of him anyway, whether years away or only days.)

Several years ago I had the great honor of being introduced to LTG. (Ret.) William G. Boykin by our mutual friend, Stu Weber. For years, Stu had told me about Jerry Boykin. Now you should know that Stu is a pastor in Oregon and a former Green Beret who was awarded three bronze stars for his service in Vietnam. Jerry Boykin, now retired, is the former commander of the United States Special Forces and a founding member of Delta Force.

In his remarkable book, *Never Surrender*, Boykin describes the unique mission of Delta Force:

> In some ways, this was a counterintuitive approach to military ops: no credit, no glory, no ticker-tape parades. There would be no public awards ceremonies or receptions. Our names would not appear in the newspapers. Success would be celebrated and stories swapped only privately, among an inner circle of special ops and intel professionals already privy to information about SCI-level (Sensitive Compartmental Information) missions. In fact, the Pentagon did not officially acknowledge our existence. After Delta began, a standard search of military personnel records for a "William G. Boykin" would reveal that no man with that name served in the United States Army.[5]

Men who are willing to serve and die without a press agent beating the drum for their exploits are men who exhibit "authentic ambition."

Arsenic Ambition

This second kind of ambition is pure rat poison, and it is defined in James 3:13–17. It's not an ambition that is zealous to honor God; it's an ambition that is demonic and opposed to God's honor. And it can get into the heart of Christians!

Note what's happening in this passage. Not only are there two kinds of ambition, but also there are two kinds of wisdom—a wisdom that comes from God and a wisdom that is demonic. In describing the demonic kind of wisdom, James will refer to "selfish ambition." That's the rat poison.

Who is wise and understanding among you? Let him show it by his good life, by deeds done in the humility that comes from wisdom. But if you harbor bitter envy and selfish ambition in your hearts, do not boast about it or deny the truth. Such "wisdom" does not come down from heaven but is earthly, unspiritual, of the devil. For where you have envy and selfish ambition, there you find disorder and every evil practice.

But the wisdom that comes from heaven is first of all pure; then peace-loving, considerate, submissive, full of mercy and good fruit, impartial and sincere. (NIV)

The root meaning of selfish ambition is "selfishness and rivalry."[6] This is an ambition that only has one thought: *What's in it for me?* It is a complete and total self-interest. It's the need to be in control in order to get your own way—a desire to be seen and viewed as superior to others. I heard Bill Lawrence one time describe it as "the need to lead."

Do you see how different this is from Paul's ambition? His ambition was to please the Lord. The idea of Paul's ambition is "to devote oneself zealously to a cause"—and his cause was to please and honor the Lord.

The wrong kind of ambition also is zealously devoted to a cause—and that is the promotion and glorification of self! James said that this kind of (demonic) wisdom and selfish ambition leads to "disorder and every evil practice."

Stop and chew for a minute on that phrase "disorder and every evil practice." A person operating in the grip of selfish ambition leaves a wake of disorder, chaos, confusion, and even anarchy behind him. That's what these individuals create all around them as they seek to get their own way. That's a demonic kind of wisdom. A man or woman running on this toxic operating system really doesn't care who gets hurt around them—as long as they get what they're after.

On the other hand, James says, the wisdom that comes down from above "is first pure, then peaceable, gentle, reasonable, full of mercy and good fruits, unwavering, without hypocrisy" (3:17 NASB). In other words, this kind of wisdom and ambition that wants to please the Lord is characterized by good behavior (3:13).

So do you see how critical it is to have the right kind of ambition? There are Christian people and Christian ministers who will do anything to get their way, achieve an agenda, and promote themselves. And if you don't believe that, check out Philippians 1:15–17, where the apostle lays it on the table and mentions the preachers who are preaching the gospel out of strife, envy, and selfish ambition.

These men are willing to do anything to get to the top.

If you ever find yourself inclined in that direction, you'd better pay attention to that flashing red light on the instrument panel of your soul. It reads: "Therefore let him who thinks he stands take heed lest he fall" (1 Cor. 10:12 NKJV).

It's dangerous territory—for any of us. In fact, it's a mine field. No man can give himself over to unrestrained self-promotion and remain spiritually unscathed. Sooner or later, you'll step on a mine, wounding both yourself and anyone else who happens to be nearby.

That's why you let God promote you.

In His way, in His time, in His will.

You don't have to do anything that is illegitimate to get a promotion. If you're in civil service and the opportunity comes along to test for a promotion, then by all means take the test. That's certainly legitimate. But make sure you don't cheat on the test—that's what you call illegitimate and illegal. So study hard and take the test, knowing as you do that your promotion or non-promotion at that moment of your life is ultimately in God's hand.

There was no civil service exam for Moses' replacement. And Joshua was smart enough not to seek it. It was just too lofty to scheme after. If the Lord brought it along, then fine. But there's no reason to manipulate and plot to become number one.

The thought of obtaining a high position can be very appealing and exciting. Philippe Petit took six years of his life to plan a promotion that would take him to the very top. And after seventy-two months of intense planning and strategizing, Petit, with the help of a small number of friends, used a bow and arrow to shoot a line from the north tower of the Twin Towers to the south tower. Working carefully and swiftly, they first attached ropes and then a 450-foot steel cable across the span on the two buildings. They rigged guylines to keep the steel cable from swaying in the wind. All of this necessary equipment had been smuggled onto a freight elevator and stored on the 104th floor the day before.

On August 7, 1974, shortly after 7:15 a.m., without hesitation, Petit stepped off the south tower and onto his 3/4" 6×19 IWRC steel cable. The twenty-four-year-old Petit made eight crossings between the still-unfinished towers, a quarter mile above the sidewalks of Manhattan, in an event that lasted about forty-five minutes. During that time, in addition to walking, he sat on the wire, gave a knee salute and, while lying on the wire, spoke with a gull circling above his head.

Port Authority Police Sergeant Charles Daniels, who had been dispatched to the roof to bring Petit down, later reported his experience:

> I observed the tightrope "dancer"—because you couldn't call him a "walker"—approximately halfway between the two towers. And upon seeing us he started to smile and laugh and he started going into a dancing routine on the high wire.... And when he got to the building we asked him to get off the high wire but instead he turned around and ran back out into the middle.... He was bouncing

up and down. His feet were actually leaving the wire
and then he would resettle back on the wire again....
Unbelievable really ... everybody was spellbound in the
watching of it.[7]

Why were people spellbound? Well, most would never attempt such a
thing in their wildest imagination. Why not? Because, "let him who thinks
he stands take heed lest he fall."

Only Petit didn't take heed. For nearly an hour he didn't take heed. He
not only thought that he could stand, he thought that he could dance. And
he had no trouble running across that cable like a squirrel. The amazing
thing is that he pulled it off.

But you have to be a little insane to even give it a thought. But maybe
Petit, like Lawrence of Arabia, isn't "in complete harmony with the normal"
(to borrow Churchill's description).

Normal people would be afraid.

"Philippe Petit says he is never afraid when he is actually on the wire.
But he always tastes a tang of fear around it. And often, after he has completed a walk, when he is on the ground, with the crew and the mayor and
a glass of champagne, he will look up and be filled with terror by what he
has just done."[8]

So maybe he is normal after all.

Petit admitted feeling a "tang of fear" after he had completed one of
his stunts. Maybe that's because all around the wire is nothing but thin
air.

Enough of Petit—let's get back to the high wire of promotion.

The problem with the high wire of promotion is that you can lose your
balance—you can lose your way—and it's a very *narrow* way on any high
wire. There's not much room for error. Now do you see why you have to do
a gut check about promotion?

Afraid of Heights

That's why Joshua didn't seek to be promoted to the top spot in Israel. It was a high and lofty promotion, and Joshua had the brains to be afraid of it. Forty years of waiting has a way of keeping your feet on the ground.

We have all seen men who have been promoted and then, in a very short time, seem to lose their way and take a great fall.

When a promotion comes our way, we're about to get a taste of new heights. But the question is—how does a man keep his balance so that he can find his way? How in the world is a man to avoid arsenic ambition and stay on a course motivated by authentic ambition? That is no easy task—but it can be done if you have the right equipment.

When a man is in new territory, he needs two things:

- He needs a compass.
- He needs a map.

We've spoken already of Delta Force, that elite Special Forces unit founded in 1977—so secret that most senators and congressmen didn't even know of its existence. It was conceived and launched by Colonel Charlie Beckwith, a Special Forces legend. Beckwith had taken a fifty-caliber straight in the belly—and lived. He invited 118 select soldiers to try out for something he couldn't tell them about. Nineteen made the brutal cut. And in the final gut-wrenching, sleep-deprived, torturous endurance test, Jerry Boykin finished first. But an army psychologist recommended that he be turned down for Delta Force. The psych believed that Boykin relied too much on God and not enough on himself. Beckwith overrode the psych and Jerry Boykin was one the original nineteen elite in Delta Force.

When Boykin showed up at the secret camp with the 117 soldiers, he didn't find what he expected. "I had envisioned a lot of tests involving shooting, close-quarters combat, and clandestine insertions. But after a pretty demanding physical training test, we found that this top secret selection course involved … walking around in the mountains. Just land navigation, and lots of it, using a simple map and a compass while carrying a heavy rucksack. There has to be more to it than this, I thought. There wasn't. But what there was, there was more than enough."[9]

For weeks and weeks, Boykin and the other men had to demonstrate that they could get anywhere in the freezing, snowy back country of North Carolina by just using a compass and a basic map. Each morning they would be given a rendezvous point, and they had to get there in a certain amount of time. They couldn't get help from any of the soldiers. They went through icy streams and had to navigate the dense hardwood forests while they carried their rifle, their rucksack, and their load-bearing gear.

The guys who couldn't use the compass and the map to get to the destination were drummed out. It was a basic skill that was required for membership in Delta Force. If a man couldn't use a compass and a map to get where he needed to be, he could never be useful to the Force. And he could certainly never be trusted to lead others in special ops.

The Compass

In the Christian life, the compass is the same for every man: *"Take up your cross and follow Me."* The Lord Jesus is True North. Just as a hiker uses true north as a reference point for every step he takes, so the believer calibrates his life to Christ. He is our aim and focus. We want to know Him and we are following Him. A man in the wilderness without a compass will fix his eyes on a marker up ahead and follow that landmark. He is our Landmark, He is our Compass, and He is our True North. We fix our eyes on Him (Heb. 12:2). He is our Commander in Chief.

That was certainly true for Joshua. Later in life, he summed up his life philosophy in a few simple words: "As for me and my house, we will serve the LORD" (Josh. 24:15). Joshua uttered those words toward the end of his years, but it had been the compass that had guided him through all of life. It got him through forty years of waiting, and one long, long season of non-events. He was following the Lord—period.

He not only had the Lord, he had a God-given map with three crucial coordinates, as we saw in Joshua 1:1–9:

- Be strong and take courage: You have His promise.
- Be strong and take courage: You have His Word.
- Be strong and take courage: You have His presence.

Three times God tells Joshua to be strong and courageous. Now why did the Lord do that? He did it because Joshua was smart enough to be scared of taking on this huge promotion and responsibility. F. B. Meyer focuses in on the situation:

> When ... the call came to him to assume the office that Moses was vacating, his heart failed him, and he needed every kind of encouragement and stimulus, both from God and man. "Be strong," means that he felt weak; "Be of good courage," means that he was frightened. "Be not dismayed" means that he seriously considered whether he would have to give up the task....
>
> It is when men are in this condition that God approaches them with the summons to undertake vast and overwhelming responsibilities. Most of us are too strong for Him to use, we are too full of our own schemes, and plans, and ways of doing things. He must empty us,

and humble us, and then He will raise us up, and make us as the rod of His strength. The world talks of the survival of the fittest. But God gives power to the faint, and increases might to those who have no strength.[10]

Did Joshua have the stuff to lead? Sure he did. He had proven himself in battle, and he had been faithful and true over the long haul of many years. But he was also acutely aware of his own weaknesses and failings. And we've all got them. A wise man understands that he is his greatest enemy. An honest man knows his record of failures and broken promises. Yes, we know that we have abilities, but the wise man knows of his great weaknesses and how easily he could fall. That's why Joshua recoiled from the promotion. He was a wise man.

But Meyer is right. God takes men who know that they are weak—and He makes them strong. And by the way, if you think you are strong and you have what it takes, He will make you weak and show you your absolute need for Him. "Apart from Me," the Lord Jesus said, "you can do nothing" (John 15:5 NASB).

King Uzziah was one of the greatest rulers in the history of Israel and Judah. His remarkable achievements and exploits are recorded for all the world to read in 2 Chronicles 26. Victory after victory, accomplishment after accomplishment—the man was a wonder. But his story ends with these words: "Hence his fame spread afar, for he was marvelously helped until he was strong" (v. 15 NASB). Those words send a chill down my spine every time I read them. *He was marvelously helped until he was strong.* When he got strong, he didn't need the Lord. And he tragically went down in flames.

Uzziah achieved beyond his wildest dreams. He was considered one of the all-time great good-guy kings. But when he got up there in the high elevations, he went down. "Therefore let him who thinks he stands take heed lest he fall."

This is why Joshua needed a map with three coordinates. If he carefully followed the compass and the map he would get the job done. So let's take the three coordinates one by one.

Be Strong and Take Courage: You Have His Promise

God has never failed to fulfill a promise. Not ever. At the end of his life, Joshua made this statement: "And now I am about to go the way of all the earth, and you know in your hearts and souls, all of you, that not one word has failed of all the good things that the LORD your God promised concerning you. All have come to pass for you; not one of them has failed" (Josh. 23:14).

Joshua 21:45 (NASB) makes the same point: "Not one of the good promises which the LORD had made to the house of Israel failed; all came to pass."

Joshua could be strong instead of weak and courageous instead of fearful because he had God's promise that God would give them victory. All he needed to do was to be obedient and keep following the Lord.

But what if you're not obedient?

Get obedient!

Right now. Quit the sin. Drop it like something hot that's searing the skin on your hand. Turn from it and look immediately to the Lord, asking for His forgiveness from your heart. That's what you do. Get obedient! This isn't rocket science. Do what you're supposed to do. Follow Christ. Do it His way, not your way.

God promises to make a way for us. But if we run from Him and from His truth, He will discipline us. And when He does, when you experience His discipline, whatever that may involve, get back in line and get out your compass. Keep your eyes on the Lord and follow Him.

I was reading Psalm 28 recently. Note the promise that God makes in verses 8–9 (NASB):

> The LORD is their strength,
> And He is a saving defense to His anointed.
> Save Your people and bless Your inheritance;
> Be their shepherd also, and carry them forever.

I see four promises here.

- He promises to be my strength.
- He promises to be a saving defense.
- He promises to shepherd me.
- He promises to carry me all the way through life.

That's pretty good stuff. For the last two days, I've been focusing on the promise that He is my saving defense. I need to know that right now in my life. And I also need to know that He will carry me forever. Not over the next ninety days, or until some contract or warranty expires, but forever.

That's not a hope, it's a promise. For that reason, I'm going to keep getting up every morning, strapping on my helmet, and heading into battle, *knowing* that He's my saving defense, and that He will carry me through.

Be Strong and Take Courage: You Have His Word

For nearly a month, the soldiers invited to the Delta Force tryout had been pushed to the point of exhaustion. They were cold, wet, and nearly freezing after hiking hundreds of miles through the North Carolina mountains, and their feet looked like ground round. One morning shortly after two, they were awakened by an officer. They looked at their watches and knew this had to be the final test. It was called the Long Walk. This was designed to break the men who remained. Jerry Boykin remembers the Long Walk:

> Eight hours into the Long Walk, I hit the wall. Night had long since passed into day and I met total exhaustion. It's hard to explain the utter sucking, draining, dry reservoir feeling. It wasn't that every muscle hurt. Every fiber burned. I reached the point where the course crossed over from physical torture to mind game....
>
> For me, after thirty miles, courage and guts were just theories—abstract concepts someone invented to explain miracles. As I stumbled through the forest, each step was a mile, each mile a marathon. I would have given anything to cave in. But instead I prayed, not so much willing myself forward as trying to tap into the strength of the Lord. I prayed Scripture, especially Isaiah 40: "He gives power to the faint, and to him who has no might he increases strength."[11]

When Boykin was beyond exhaustion and running on fumes, it was the Word of God that kept him going. Joshua was told to meditate on the Word. That's very significant, and it's exactly what General Boykin did years ago on the Long Walk. Warren Wiersbe explains, "The Hebrew word translated 'meditate' means 'to mutter.' It was the practice of the Jews to read Scriptures aloud (Acts 8:26–40) and talk about it to themselves and to one another (Deut. 6:6–9). This explains why God warned Joshua that the Book of the Law (Genesis through Deuteronomy) was not to depart out of his mouth (Josh. 1:8)."[12]

Boykin muttered the Word of God to himself. He found that it was his strength, and he did not let it depart from his mouth or his mind.

If you don't know the Word, how will you know the promises? The promises are *in* the Word. You have to be reading your Bible—there's no other way to make it. But when you know the Word, then you've got the promises to get you through when the trail is dark and your strength is spent:

> Your word is a lamp to my feet
>> And a light to my path. (Ps. 119:105 NASB)

Be Strong and Take Courage: You Have His Presence

At one crucial turn in the trail after Moses had taken on the mantle of leadership for the nation, he said to the Lord, "If You don't go with us, I'm not going to do this." Moses wanted the assurance of God's presence—not some of the time but all of the time.

And this was the promise that God gave to Joshua as he was stepping into the top job: *"Just as I have been with Moses, I will be with you."* (Josh. 1:5 NASB). And then for good measure, the Lord says, *"I will not fail you or forsake you."*

Now there it is in all of its three-dimensional glory—

I will be with you.

I will not fail you.

I will not forsake you.

No wonder Joshua was bold.

No wonder he was courageous.

Go and do likewise.

Chapter Eight

The Worst Possible Time

"Whether these are the best of times or the worst of times,
it's the only time we've got."
—Art Buchwald

The Tax Reform Act of 1986 hit a lot of people very hard.

Now I realize that you probably haven't given a lot of thought in recent days to the Tax Reform Act of 1986—but there's a lesson in it for you if you desire to be used by God.

There's no need to go into the details of the bill except to say this: It significantly changed the rules for investing in real estate. And when the bill passed, it proved to be the financial ruin of thousands of investors all over the nation. For them, it couldn't have come at a worse time.

Two men living in two separate cites had their lives dramatically altered by this change in the law. Both were Christians and serious about their faith. They didn't know one another, but they both shared a deep desire to be used by God. One lived in Nashville and the other resided in Orlando—and they were both making money hand over fist.

The guy living in Nashville was twenty-six years old and a multi-millionaire. But when the Tax Reform Act of 1986 was signed into law it changed all the rules. It was sort of like playing Scrabble and then in the middle of the game the rules were changed so that you could only use words in French or Spanish. That's a big change.

As a result of this rule change, the strategy of using large debt to finance real estate deals fell apart overnight. So one morning this guy in Nashville got a call from his bank telling him they wanted him to repay millions of dollars on their note in the next ninety days. Since the Tax Reform Act caused real estate prices to crash, he couldn't make the payment and had to file for bankruptcy.

This guy had a real desire to be used by God, and he struggled to understand why God had allowed this to happen. But one thing was clear to him: He was never going to go into debt again. He began to study the Scriptures to discover what God had to say about finances, and determined in his heart to live according to those principles. He then began to casually share those principles with a few friends. These friends so benefited from his insights that they invited him to teach a class on money at their church. That in turn led him into doing financial counseling. He continued to refine and hone the biblical principles into clear and logical steps that people could follow to get a grip on their finances.

Today you can watch him every weeknight on the Fox Business News channel or hear him nationwide on Fox News Radio. He has written several best-selling books, and helped hundreds of thousands of couples and singles get out of debt and live according to biblical principles.

His name is Dave Ramsey, and it all began with the Tax Reform Act of 1986, which couldn't have come at a worse time. Or so he thought at the time.

As it turned out, it was the crisis brought on by the change in the tax code that changed his life completely and enabled him to be so greatly used by God.

The other guy in Orlando was doing the same kind of real estate deals. And remember that these were all completely legitimate under the law.

It was how the law was written and intended. But suddenly everything changed when the rules were changed. And this Christian guy in Orlando, who had one company that was one of Florida's one hundred largest privately held companies, was also the president or managing partner of fifty-nine companies and partnerships. Let's just say he was doing pretty well for himself.

And then along came the Tax Reform Act of 1986 and although he managed to stave off bankruptcy, he pretty much went down the drain just like the guy in Nashville.[1] This major setback sent him into the Scriptures as well. He was driven to find meaning in his life, now that his great wealth had all but disappeared. Out of his personal study of the Bible, he began sharing some of the truths that had helped him with some friends. Then he was asked to lead a Bible study for some men who were facing the same kinds of issues in their lives.

In 1989, Patrick Morley wrote a great book for men titled *Man in the Mirror.* Pat's books and materials developed over the years into Man in the Mirror Ministries. Hundreds of thousands of men have been impacted by Pat Morley's writing and organizational brilliance, which in turn has given birth to countless men's ministries around the world.[2]

And it all started for Pat with the Tax Reform Act of 1986 that, once again, came at the worst possible time. Pat explains it in his own words:

> When the Tax Reform Act of 1986 passed, my ambitions
> collided with the stark reality of the real estate equity mar-
> ket, or, should I say, the disappearance of the real estate
> equity market. Overnight, and I mean literally overnight,
> equity was a dead topic. No one, but no one, would talk
> to me. With many large development projects unfunded,
> I suddenly realized what I wanted simply wasn't going to
> happen.

The result? My ambition collided with God's plan for my life, and the glory days were replaced with agonizing months upon months of working out problems. People had to be laid off, expenses slashed, lenders contacted—a very humbling experience.[3]

It couldn't have come at a worse time. But out of the devastation, Morley eventually saw the realization of his desire for God to use him.

Water Crossings

Joshua and Caleb were involved in two significant crossings of water. The first was the Red Sea. That occurred just weeks before God sent the twelve spies into the land. But forty years later, after Joshua wandered and waited for all those decades in the wilderness, God told him to get the people ready to go. They were going to do another water crossing, only this time it was going to be the Jordan River.

At flood stage.

It was the worst possible time to cross the Jordan. But more on that in the next chapter. For right now, we're going to zoom in on that first water crossing at the Red Sea.

Now the danger of this Red Sea story is that we think we know it so well that there's nothing to learn from it. That's a mistake. Maybe we've seen an old TV rerun of Charlton Heston in *The Ten Commandments*, or flew over the incident at thirty thousand feet on our way through a read-the-Bible-through-in-one-year program, and so we think we have a handle on what happened.

One thing we can be sure of: We'll never grasp the full significance of that moment until we get to heaven and get some eyewitness reports.

Harold Macmillan was prime minister of England from 1957 to 1963. On one occasion he was speaking to a group of journalists, and one of those reporters asked him a pointed question.

"Mr. Prime Minister, what is the greatest challenge that a statesman faces?"

Macmillan immediately replied, "Events, my dear boy, events."

We all have events that we have put on our calendars. Christmas is an event. So is high school graduation or a wedding anniversary. These are the events that we are expecting and looking forward to.

When Macmillan spoke of "events," he wasn't referring to the *planned* events in our lives, he was speaking of the unforeseen events—the unplanned "happenings" that throw us into crisis.

It is the unforeseen events that are the greatest challenge, not only to a statesman, but also to anyone living life. It is the unforeseen events that can change our lives in an instant. Like the Tax Reform Act of 1986. When it comes to unforeseen events, you should understand three truths:

1. In your life there are no unforeseen events.

These unforeseen events may not be on your calendar, but they are definitely on the Lord's. God is not shocked by the events that shock you. He is in control of all things. Not some things—all things. God has a plan for the ages and He is a micromanager. His plan is incredibly detailed, and it includes all things. Now I know that raises questions, and in the first book of this series, *God Built*, I discussed those hard questions in detail. I won't repeat that teaching here, except to make one critical point: *God is never the author of evil.* When evil happens, God is never the author of sin. But He does *use* evil, *control* evil, and even *put it to work* for the good of His people and the glory of His name.

When Joseph confronted his brothers, looking back on their evil act of selling him into slavery at the age of seventeen, he said to them, "You intended it for evil, but God intended it for good."[4]

God was not shocked when the brothers sold Joseph into slavery. It was part of His plan from Day One—and even before that. But Joseph pinned the responsibility for the evil, not on God, but on his brothers. Could God have stopped the evil? Yes. Did He stop it? No. Why not? Because many years down the road He would turn the evil into magnificent good.

Let's not forget the main point. In your life there are unforeseen events. They may be unforeseen to you, but they are foreseen and planned by God.

2. Unforeseen events can shake us.

The unforeseen events blindside us. They shock us. And they sometimes tumble us into crisis mode.

3. Unforeseen events can shape us.

These events come into our lives for a reason. We never suffer randomly as Christians; there is always a purpose to the hardship and trial. And those hardships and trials usually come into our lives as unforeseen events—circumstances that can shock us, stun us, rattle us, and make us sick with worry.

Have you ever been sick with worry? Of course you have. You've been sick with the flu and sick with a fever, but it's much worse to be sick with worry. What would make you that worried? Nine times out of ten, it's an unforeseen event that has suddenly come streaking out of space like a meteor to crash into your backyard ... or living room.

God uses unforeseen events not just to shake us, but to *shape* us. We run into situations (or they run into us), and they're beyond our control. So we get sick with worry trying to figure out how it's ever going to work out. God *knows* how He's going to work it out—but we can't see His solution. And as we go through the pain and learn to trust Him, we develop spiritual muscle and we grow. That's the purpose of the unforeseen event. No pain—no gain.

It was Matthew Henry who observed, "God sometimes raises difficulties in the lives of His people that He may have the glory of subduing them and helping His people over them."

That's the story when it comes to the unforeseen events of our lives.

And that's the story of the Red Sea in a nutshell.

Red Sea Workout

I know that you know this story. Maybe you grew up in Sunday school and could tell the whole thing by memory. Maybe you saw that *Prince of Egypt* animated movie of Moses, and still remember how the animators put it on the big screen. Or perhaps you've read Robert J. Morgan's classic little book, *The Red Sea Rules*. I'm indebted to Morgan for his insights, and I want to pass on some of his wisdom to you in this chapter.

The thing we tend to forget is that it really happened, and real people experienced the whole thing. Joshua and Caleb were there for the whole Red Sea event. What happened at that celebrated crossroads of history was not only an unforeseen event for them, but for the entire nation.

Now, I don't intend to go exhaustively through the entire story; it's there in Exodus 13—14 in all its amazing glory for everyone to read. But I do want to make several observations that have application to anyone who wants to be used by God.

Let's simply headline the story this way:

The Red Sea was an unforeseen event that threw the people into crisis.

And under that overriding idea I want to make a very critical observation: *They found themselves in crisis because God led them into the crisis.*

Do you know those maps in the back of the Bible that you never look at? In my Bible, the second map is titled "The Exodus of Israel." It shows the route that God told Moses to take out of Egypt and into the Promised

Land. Now the Promised Land is what we know today as modern Israel. Actually the borders were larger than present-day Israel, but for now let's just say Israel as we know it.

In Exodus 13:17–18 we read some critical information:

> When Pharaoh let the people go, God did not lead them by way of the land of the Philistines, although that was near. For God said, "Lest the people change their minds when they see war and return to Egypt." But God led the people around by the way of the wilderness toward the Red Sea. And the people of Israel went up out of the land of Egypt equipped for battle.

Did you catch the fact that God did not lead them to take the shortest route? The quickest way was through the land of the Philistines. That's the way they would have gone if they'd followed MapQuest. That's the way Triple A would have sent them. If you check your map in the back of your Bible (just past the concordance, you can't miss it), you will see that the nearest route was directly up the coast of the Mediterranean Sea right into Israel. They could get on the interstate and take the scenic route. And when they got tired, they could pull off at a rest stop, get some barbecue, and enjoy the seaside view.

That was the logical way and it was the shortest way.

But God didn't take them that way.

According to verse 18, "God led the people around by the way of the wilderness toward the Red Sea." And once again, if you will check your map, you'll note that this direction made no sense. It would have been like saying, "I'm going to take you out of Texas into Chicago, but I want to go through Florida." The short way—the quickest, most convenient route to the Promised Land was a straight shot north right up the coast. But God says no—let's go southeast to the Red Sea.

And then in Exodus 14:1–2 God specifically tells Moses to have the people camp on the shore of the Red Sea.

Now here's the point: They were at the Red Sea because God specifically led them to the Red Sea. And they were about to encounter an unforeseen event that God had planned that would throw them into crisis. Therefore (and please don't miss this), God led them into the crisis.

Now let's freeze the story for a minute and ask a question: When the people of Israel were camped at the Red Sea, how were they doing? The answer is that they were doing great. Let me tell you why.

They had just come out of Egypt, where they had lived for the last 430 years. When they finally left Egypt, after God had shocked, battered, and devastated the people of that land through His ten plagues, all the rank-and-file Egyptians were delighted to see them go. So delighted, in fact, that they gave their former slaves presents of gold, silver, and precious jewels. *("Here, take whatever you want. Just go—quickly!")* So the people of Israel, who had lived as slaves without a penny to their name, left Egypt with fabulous riches (Ex. 12:35–36). For the first time in their lives, Joshua and Caleb had some serious money—and so did all the other families in Israel.

That's why they were doing so well when they camped at the Red Sea. For the first time in hundreds of years they were free—and wealthy to boot. Such a deal! They couldn't believe their good fortune. So after they had made camp, had dinner, and put the kids to bed, they went online to check their accounts at Schwab. So how were they doing? Better than they had been in hundreds of years. And they were headed to the Promised Land where God would give them houses they wouldn't have to build, wells they wouldn't have to dig, mature trees they didn't have to plant, and crops they didn't have to sow (Deut. 6:10–11).

Now watch this.

As they are camped at the Red Sea, God is up to something. What is He up to? He is about to instigate a crisis. It's all laid out in Exodus 14:1–4 (NASB):

Now the LORD spoke to Moses, saying,

"Tell the sons of Israel to turn back and camp before Pi-hahiroth, between Migdol and the sea; you shall camp in front of Baal-zephon, opposite it, by the sea.

"For Pharaoh will say of the sons of Israel, 'They are wandering aimlessly in the land; the wilderness has shut them in.' Thus I will harden Pharaoh's heart, and he will chase after them; and I will be honored through Pharaoh and all his army, and the Egyptians will know that I am the LORD." And they did so.

Did you get that? While the two million people of Israel are content and comfortable in their camp, God begins stirring up Pharaoh to come after them and bring them back into slavery. God is going to harden Pharaoh's heart and make him chase after them. It's important to understand that God hardened Pharaoh's heart because Pharaoh had continually hardened his own heart against the Lord. In spite of all that he saw of God's glory—in spite of all the mind-bending miracles performed before his own eyes—he simply refused to bow the knee before the Lord. When God hardened Pharaoh's heart, He simply let Pharaoh go the way he wanted to go—which was away from God.

So even while the people of Israel were enjoying their little camping trip at the beach, counting their treasures, and wondering how many days it would take to get to the Promised Land, God Himself was about to bring a crisis upon them. He had planned it, purposed it, and put it into motion.

And why in the world would He do that?

The answer is clearly stated in verse 4 (NASB): "Thus I will harden Pharaoh's heart, and he will chase after them; and I will be honored through Pharaoh and all his army, and the Egyptians will know that I am the LORD."

God brought about the crisis so that *His name might be honored.*[5]

Just so it can't be missed, He states His purpose two more times in verses 17–18. He is doing all of this so that *His name might be honored.*

God wants His name to be honored.

Jesus said in Matthew 6:9,

> Pray then like this,
>> Our Father in heaven,
>> hallowed be your name.

The word *hallowed* means to honor or reverence. In other words, Jesus said that we are to pray that God's name would be honored. And yet every day we hear God's name taken in vain. We hear His name mocked and blasphemed.

We're told, "Don't bring His name into our schools. Don't bring His name into Congress. Don't bring His name into the marketplace."

Psalm 9:10 (NASB) says "those who know Your name will put their trust in You."

Proverbs 18:10 (NASB) declares that "the name of the LORD is a strong tower; the righteous runs into it and is safe."

God wants His name to be *honored.* That's why He has led Israel to the Red Sea, where they are about to experience an unforeseen event that absolutely panics them. And when they get panicked and realize there is no escape, they will cry out to God, He will deliver them, and His name will be *honored.*

Exodus 14:10 gives the play-by-play as Israel suddenly sees Pharaoh's army and six hundred chariots come out of nowhere:

"When Pharaoh drew near, the people of Israel lifted up their eyes, and behold, the Egyptians were marching after them, and they feared greatly. And the people of Israel cried out to the LORD."

It was the worst possible time for Pharaoh's army to show up, because there was no escape. There was literally no way out.

Keil and Delitzsch describe the vise grip:

> When the Israelites saw the advancing army of the
> Egyptians, they were greatly alarmed; for their situation
> to human eyes was a very unfortunate one. Shut in on the
> east by the sea, on the south and west by high mountains,
> and with the army of the Egyptians behind them, destruc-
> tion seemed inevitable, since they were neither outwardly
> armed nor inwardly prepared for a successful battle.[6]

So what did the people do in their panic and fear?

They cried out.

There is a distinct difference in the Scriptures between praying and
crying out. Crying out is a prayer of absolute desperation. It is an audible,
out-loud plea to God for help. It's not the prayer you pray over dinner. It is
a prayer of desperation—because if God doesn't come through and answer
you, you are finished. That's what it means to cry out.

As I described in the previous pages, I cried out to God after I was suddenly removed from my ministry position, as I walked the back streets of
my neighborhood. I cried out loud, not really caring who heard me, asking
God to make a way financially. And within two hours, I had a phone call
with His answer.

But then I had to cry out all over again, as we faced yet another impossible situation.

Take Two

"This is the worst possible time to be selling a house," my friend told me.

That wasn't what I wanted to hear at that moment.

Commenting on the state of real estate in our community, he went on to say, "The average house in this town is on the market for eighteen to twenty-four months."

Those words gave me a sick feeling in my stomach. As I told you in a previous chapter, I had experienced the abrupt closing of a chapter in my life that I had imagined was going to continue for a while.

God had taken the immediate financial pressure off by providing the insurance check. And as I mentioned, I'd never had that much money in the bank in my life. But it had become very clear to Mary and me that we needed to move, since my new career would involve quite a bit of cross-country traveling. It seemed that the Lord was leading us to Dallas. We had friends and some family there, and Dallas had a great airport that would get me to either coast in three hours.

On the heels of our remarkable financial provision in the form of the check from the insurance company, we faced another testing of our faith. Now I have related this story in one of my earlier books, but I think you will soon see why it bears repeating.

The abrupt ending had happened in February, and it was our goal to sell the house and get moved to Dallas by the time school started in August. So we put our four-bedroom home on the market, feeling upbeat and optimistic about it all.

But the days went by ... quite a few of them. And we'd had only one showing in sixty days. The economy was bad, the market was sluggish, and it didn't look good for us to get to Dallas by August. So we began to pray that God would make a way. If He could provide nearly half a year's income in one check, He could certainly get us to Dallas.

A few days later I was in a barbecue joint eating a sandwich and overheard a real estate broker in the next booth telling his friend that there were no four-bedroom houses in our area for rent. Well, I made a few calls and it turned out that real estate broker was on target. So then I thought about renting our house. I really didn't want to do that, but if we could rent out the house on a good lease, it might be the best way to go in this tight market. And then when I thought "lease," I thought "maybe we could do a lease with an option to buy." Mary and I talked and prayed about it and decided to give it a try. Now remember, we hadn't had any action for sixty days and the clock was ticking. We needed to move and get on with the next chapter of life.

So I put an ad in the paper indicating we had a four-bedroom for rent and would consider an option to buy. We also put in the ad that we would hold an open house on Sunday afternoon from one to five. The ad came out on Saturday, and that afternoon we got a call from a couple asking if they could come over and take a look. I recognized the man as the owner of a barbecue restaurant that I regularly visited. They looked around the house and indicated that they would like to take it. They were headed out of town, but would be back on Monday and we could sign the one-year lease then.

We were thrilled. We could now make plans to move. Officially unstuck after several months of waiting, it now looked like we would finally be on our way. Several hours later, however, the couple's son called and indicated his parents had changed their minds and wouldn't be leasing the house after all.

At that moment, the call hit me like a kick in the gut. We had experienced the thrill of victory, and now we had to deal with the agony of defeat. I have to admit that I was very discouraged as I went to bed that night, and had difficulty falling asleep. I just couldn't understand why God had allowed that to happen.

The open house was still on for Sunday afternoon. Mary took the kids down to the neighborhood pool and I stayed at the house, hoping someone would come by. Shortly after lunch, I got a call asking for directions to the house. About thirty minutes later there was a knock at the door. There stood a very nice-looking family—a father and mother and three little stair-step kids. I invited them in and told them to please look around as much as they wanted. I was watching the Masters golf tournament, but would be happy to answer any questions.

Maybe ten minutes later the guy, Scott, came downstairs and said, "Steve, are you a Christian? I saw your study Bible on your desk upstairs."

I indicated that I was and he told me he knew the Lord as well. We got acquainted for a few minutes and then he said, "My wife loves this house. It's absolutely perfect for us. I'm just finishing up my medical residency, and I'm joining a practice here in town. I don't have the money right now to buy your house, but I'd like to lease it for a year and then we could buy it. You mentioned in your ad a lease with option to buy. How does that work?"

"I honestly don't know," I replied, "but I bet you that we can find someone who can help us work it out."

I told him the price and he said that sounded good to him. So we shook hands and we had a deal. They would lease the house for a year and then buy it outright.

Before they left, we all gathered in the family room and prayed. They had been praying for months and we had been praying for months. And now the Lord had worked things out for both families. We were all very grateful to the Lord as we shook hands and the kids piled into their minivan.

I was pumped! Now I was thanking God that the other couple had pulled out. They just wanted a one-year lease. Now I had a one-year lease with a sale! Thank You, Lord! I can't tell you how relieved I was.

About an hour later, the phone rang and it was Scott. "Hey, Steve, I was just talking with my pastor and telling him about the house. He's my best friend as well as my pastor, and I was wondering if you'd mind if we ran back over so I could show him the house."

"Sure, come on over. I'm just watching the Masters."

So thirty minutes later, Scott showed up with his pastor. They looked around, we talked for a while, and then we prayed again, thanking God for His great answer to prayer.

About an hour later, the phone rang again.

"Hey, Steve. I'm sorry to bother you again, but would it be a great bother for my wife to come back and bring the pastor's wife? They really are our best friends, and they're so excited, and my wife would really love to see the house again."

"Come on over, I'm still here watching golf, and Mary is still at the pool with the kids."

Within a few minutes, the whole group of them pulled up in the driveway. They all looked around again, we talked quite a bit, and even figured out that we had mutual friends—it was just a great time. And then we all joined hands and prayed again. I asked them if they had a Sunday-night service, because if they did, maybe they should just bring the entire congregation over. It was really quite an afternoon.

So they left, and ten minutes later Mary walked in with the kids.

"How did it go?" she asked. "Did anyone come by?"

"Well, I leased the house for a year and then they're going to buy it at our asking price, plus we had three prayer meetings, and a revival broke out."

I got Mary caught up on the details of what had just transpired, and we just looked at each other and laughed. And don't forget, just the night before I had trouble going to sleep because I was so disappointed that the other couple had canceled on us. Now I was thanking God that they had canceled!

The next day we went to Chili's for lunch to celebrate. We needed to not only celebrate what God had done, but we needed to think through our next steps now that we had the house leased.

As we were being shown to our table, a guy eating lunch said, "Hi, Steve. How are you?"

I recognized this man because we had mutual friends from another church. But I didn't know his name or what he did.

"I hear you're moving to Dallas."

"Yes, we're excited about it."

And then he said, "That's great. Have you sold your house yet?"

"Well, I just leased it to a young doctor. We're doing a lease with an option to buy in twelve months. He's joining a medical practice here in town."

He paused for a minute and said, "May I ask his name?"

I told him the name and he said, "Steve, he's coming to work for *me*. He's joining my practice."

I said, "No kidding. Why don't you give him a raise so he can buy my house!"

We all laughed and we went on to our table.

The next night I got a call and it was Scott.

"Hey, Steve. I've got some great news. I've got the down payment to buy your house! We don't need to do the lease!"

I could hardly believe my ears.

"Scott, that's great. Wow! That's actually unbelievable. So what happened?

"Well, didn't you run into Tom yesterday at Chili's?"

I was astonished. "Yes, I did."

"Well, he called me and asked me about the house and I told him that my wife loved it. He said if that was the house she wanted, they would go ahead and advance the money for a down payment. That way we could get the house and you could get on your way to Dallas with your house sold."

I was absolutely dumbfounded. Flummoxed. Stunned.

It had been the worst possible time to be selling a four-bedroom house. But God stepped in and took care of it. We didn't wait eighteen months and we didn't wait twenty-four months, like other people in town were doing. Our house was sold!

And God did it.

Now do you know why I tell that story? Because God's name is honored by that story. I was in crisis, and He had led me into the crisis. It was an impossible situation with no solution. But God brought about the crisis and delivered me, so that His name might be honored.

That's a day that I will never forget. It was on that day that God came through for us. Even though my kids were young when that happened, they know the story very well. One day they will be telling that story to their kids. And God's name will be honored in the next generation

Who knows? Maybe the Lord is setting *you* up for a story that will honor His name. And many years after you have exited this earth, your grandchildren will still be talking about it.

God never wastes a crisis.

Chapter Nine

Fighting Off Fear

"Trials are the ballast of life."
—Old English Proverb

od likes men. In fact, He invented men.

It's a sad truth, however, that not every male is manly, even though that would be God's desire. This contemporary culture doesn't value manliness. In many cases, manliness is despised.

Harvey C. Mansfield is a professor at Harvard. But don't hold that against him. He has written a book that actually makes sense, a most unusual occurrence among Harvard professors these days. The book is titled *Manliness,* and it's a wonder Mansfield didn't get fired for writing it. After all, manliness is something that is no longer valued throughout American culture. Mansfield describes the problem:

> Today the very word manliness seems quaint and obsolete. We are in the process of making the English language gender-neutral, and manliness, the quality of one gender, or rather, of one sex, seems to describe the essence of the enemy we are attacking, the evil we are eradicating. Recently I had a call from the alumni magazine at the university where I work, asking me to comment on a former

professor of mine now being honored. Responding too quickly, I said: "What impressed all of us about him was his manliness." There was silence on the other end of the line, and finally the female voice said, "Could you think of another word?"

We now avoid using "man" to refer to both sexes, as in the glowing phrase "rights of man" to which America was once dedicated. All the man-words have been brought to account and corrected. Mankind has become humankind; man of the year, person of the year; and so on. But even when "man" means only male, "manly" seems to be pretentious in our new society, and threatening to it as well. A manly man is making a point of the bad attitude he ought to be playing down.

The attempt to make our language gender-neutral reveals something of the ambition of our democracy today. A gender-neutral language implies a gender-neutral society, making a pervasive change in the way we live our lives. Our society has adopted, quite without realizing the magnitude of the change, a practice of equality between the sexes that has never been known before in all human history.[1]

And then Mansfield gives a bottom-line description of manliness: "Manliness, like suffering, deals with fear. The Greek word for manliness, *andreia*, is also the word the Greeks used for courage, the virtue concerned with controlling fear…. Manly men rise above their fear, but in doing so they carry their fear with them, though it is under control."[2]

Fear is always with us. That's because we are never completely free of the giants. As I write these words, our American economy seems to be in free fall. The government keeps trying to fix it, and they can't. But that doesn't keep them from printing more money and throwing it into the system. This economic downturn is like a runaway virus that can't be stopped. Banks keep failing, prices keep going up, and real estate keeps plunging. We haven't seen fear like this since the days of the Great Depression.

Maybe that's why a white blues singer from California is so big in England right now. His name is Seasick Steve, and his most popular song is "I Started Out With Nothin' and I Still Got Most of It Left."[3]

A lot of men could be singing that song these days, because it describes their current situation and immediate future. These are fearful times. But for those who know God and His ironclad promises, we must make sure that we fight to keep our fears under control.

Manly Men of God

In 1 Corinthians 16:13 (NASB), God says, "Be on the alert, stand firm in the faith, act like men, be strong."

Our culture doesn't want men to act like men.

But God does.

God always wants His men to act like men—even when they are in a culture that despises masculinity.

Joshua had been given the responsibility to take two million people across the Jordan River and into the Promised Land. In order to do so, he was going to have to:

- be on the alert;
- stand firm in the faith;
- act like a man;
- be strong.

If you want to be used by God, those four commands make up your job description.

We must be on the alert because Satan is a roaring lion who roams about the earth, seeking whom he may devour.[4] When a man gets serious about Christ, the Enemy gets serious about that man. He will do everything he can to bring you down. So you must be on constant guard against "the schemes of the devil" (Eph. 6:11).

We must stand firm in the faith because that's the very essence of the Christian life. We can't see what's up ahead, so we walk by faith, not by sight. For His part, God constantly places us in situations that overwhelm us, where we can't even imagine how we'll get through. We don't know how it's going to work out, because we can't put all of the pieces together. That's where faith comes in. Our faith is in our Father and His promises. He will make a way when we can't see a way.

We must act like men because these circumstances in which we find ourselves often have the potential to bring much harm and destruction to our lives, our careers, and our families. But even though we may feel afraid, we don't cut and run—we manage our fear and hold it down and keep moving ahead, all the while trusting in our Father to give us what we need at the exact right moment.

That's what it means to "be strong." We live life as Christian men according to the words of Ephesians 6:10: "Be strong in the Lord and in the strength of his might."

Now Joshua had to apply all of these commands when the forty-year wait was over, and he stepped into the role of leadership. After four weary decades of wandering and waiting because of the unfaithfulness of the ten spies, it was time for a new generation to lay aside that bad example of their fathers and move out in faith, trusting God to give them victory.

In order to do so, they would need to *be on the alert, stand firm in the faith, act like men, and be strong.*

A new generation of men was about to be tested, to see if they could be manly and faithful. Joshua 3:1–6 gives us the context and setting:

> Then Joshua rose early in the morning and they set out from Shittim. And they came to the Jordan, he and all the people of Israel, and lodged there before they passed over. At the end of three days the officers went through the camp and commanded the people, "As soon as you see the ark of the covenant of the LORD your God being carried by the Levitical priests, then you shall set out from your place and follow it. Yet there shall be a distance between you and it, about 2,000 cubits in length. Do not come near it, in order that you may know the way you shall go, for you have not passed this way before." Then Joshua said to the people, "Consecrate yourselves, for tomorrow the LORD will do wonders among you." And Joshua said to the priests, "Take up the ark of the covenant and pass on before the people." So they took up the ark of the covenant and went before the people.

There are *five* observations we need to make from this pivotal event in the life of Joshua and Israel.

1. He commanded them to cross—at the worst possible time.

Here we go again! Another key event, another strategic moment in the history of Israel, and it's taking place at the worst possible time. Why does this keep coming up? Because God keeps leading us into the precise situations where He can best demonstrate His greatness to us.

Why was this the worst possible time? We're given a pretty strong clue in Joshua 4:19 (NASB): "Now the people came up from the Jordan on the tenth of the first month and camped at Gilgal on the eastern edge of Jericho."

So what's the clue? The clue is the date. It was the tenth day of the first month. Now to us that means it was January. But they had a different calendar, and it wasn't the dead of winter; it was in springtime. The first month for them was in the middle of harvest season. And here's another clue: Harvest season was a bad time to cross the Jordan River, "for the Jordan overflows all its banks all the days of harvest" (Josh. 3:15 NASB).

In other words, he commanded them to cross when the Jordan was at flood stage. Paul Enns put the clues together when he writes, "In the springtime the normally narrow river flooded its banks so that it filled the depression valley that was 150 feet deep and as much as a mile wide."[5]

That's what you call the deep end of the pool.

It was the worst possible time. I've had the privilege of baptizing my son, Josh, and my daughter, Rachel, in the Jordan River, and I can tell you that the river wasn't a mile wide and 150 feet deep. We were there in July and the river was four or five feet deep and maybe fifty yards across. That would have been a good time for the people to cross the river. But God wanted them to cross at flood stage, to show them His greatness and His power. So God said to Joshua, take the people and cross over.

The instructions were very clear. They were to ford the river—not by cabin cruiser or Jet Skis, but on foot. They were to walk three thousand feet behind the ark of the covenant.

So why did God want them to cross at the worst possible time? To bring honor to His name. "What I am doing you do not understand now, but afterward you will understand" (John 13:7).

Nearly three hundred years ago, William Cowper wrote one of the greatest hymns ever penned. The title is "God Moves in a Mysterious Way." The first verse reads:

> God moves in a mysterious way
>> His wonders to perform;
>> He plants His footsteps in the sea
>> And rides upon the storm.
> Deep in unfathomable mines
>> Of never-failing skill
>> He treasures up His bright designs
>> And works His sovereign will.

Why did God command them to cross at the worst possible time? Did it make sense to them at the time? Probably not—and that's because God's ways are mysterious. But He knows what He's doing, and He knows what is best. So many times, we don't know either of those things. But He does. That's why God often asks us to obey Him at the worst possible time.

Part of what He's doing is testing our manliness, to see if we will fight off the fear and trust Him completely. It was C. H. Spurgeon who said, "When we cannot trace God's hand we can trust God's heart."

Now when they crossed at flood stage, they actually could trace God's hand. As they kept their commanded distance, Joshua 3:4 (NIV) indicates that "then you will know which way to go." As the ark was carried ahead of them, it literally made the road they were to follow. God marked out the path ahead of them—right through an impossibility.

2. He commanded them to camp—and contemplate the impossible.

For three days every man, woman, and child in the nation of Israel was camped along the banks of that river. The parents watched the little kids very closely, because if one of them fell into the brown swirling water of that river, the child would be drowned in an instant.

Every waking hour for three days, they looked at that raging killer of a river, and thought, *This is the worst possible time to cross this thing.*

In other words, they were in another crisis. God had given them an impossible task. They were being asked to do something that—like the flooding river—was way over their heads and way beyond their means. But to put the cards on the table, they were in crisis because, once again, God had *led* them into the crisis. He had created the crisis, just as He did for their parents at the Red Sea forty years earlier.

Now as we have seen, God miraculously opened the Red Sea and took them across. As they were crossing, the cloud that led them by day moved behind them and descended on Pharaoh's army, plunging them into darkness and confusion. After they had crossed to the other side, God lifted the darkness and gave Pharaoh a clear path to pursue them. And as they pursued, the waters that God held back for Israel were now released, wiping Pharaoh and his crack Egyptian troops from the planet.

Now the amazing thing to me is that just weeks later, the twelve spies are commissioned to go into the Promised Land. And as we have seen, ten of those men were "notable," because they convinced the people that they were not able to take on the giants.

What had they learned about God from the Red Sea miracle?

Nothing. Nada. Zero.

They refused to apply the truth they had seen with their own eyes to the very next crisis that crossed their path—which happened to be "giants in the land."

What are a few giants to a God who can open up a path through the sea and walk His people through the middle of it on dry land? What are a few nine-foot freaks with spears to the God who can draw an opposing army into the middle of the sea, then close it in over their heads?

Am I missing something here? Doesn't it follow logically that if God could do one mighty, earth-shaking miracle, He could do a few more?

Yes, it does.

But the entire house of Israel had refused to apply the truth. As a result, every one of them died in an empty wilderness of unbelief, except for Joshua and Caleb. And now the children of those who died were about to get their turn to trust God and apply their faith.

3. He commanded the leaders to go first—to demonstrate their faith.

Did you ever flunk a course in college? I did, and I remember it well.

It was meteorology, of all things.

Meteorology is the scientific study of the earth's atmosphere, especially its patterns of climate and weather. Well, to be honest, I was nineteen years old and I wasn't planning on being a TV weatherman. So I fooled around and flunked the course. And it was an "F" that I richly deserved.

When you flunk a course with the Lord, however, you're going to have to go to summer school and make it up. Or in the case of Israel at the Jordan, they were going to flood-stage school. Allow me to explain. In Joshua 3:12 (NIV), God says to Joshua, "Now then, take for yourselves twelve men from each of the tribes of Israel, one man for each tribe."

Now where have we heard that before? If I'm not mistaken it was in Numbers 13, when God told Moses to pick twelve men, one from each tribe, to go on a mission to check out the land. Ten of the twelve, as we have already seen, flunked the course. Now it was time to take the course over.

Once again, twelve men are to be picked, one from each tribe. At this point, God gives no reason for their selection. God simply tells Joshua, go ahead and pick your team of twelve. (We'll meet these guys in a minute.)

God then gives clear instructions that the priests (the Levites) are to carry the ark and step into the raging floodwaters. And the moment that their feet touch the water, the waters will roll back just as the Red Sea rolled back. The Levites were the spiritual leaders of the nation, and there is a principle here: *Leaders are to lead by their example.*

The spiritual shepherds of Israel were to be men of faith, and that meant they went into the water first. They didn't wait for a woman of faith to go first. These guys were manly, and they were willing to prove it by putting themselves on the line. Once again, William Cowper said it best:

> Ye fearful saints, fresh courage take;
>> The clouds ye so much dread
>> Are big with mercy and shall break
>> In blessings on your head.
> Judge not the Lord by feeble sense,
>> But trust Him for His grace;
>> Behind a frowning providence
>> He hides a smiling face.

4. He commanded the leaders to stay in harm's way.

So the Levites take the ark and go into the water first. And then they are commanded to go halfway across and stand there, waiting for the rest of the folks to cross over.

That's called applying your faith.

If that water gave way at any moment, they would immediately join Charlie the Tuna. But it didn't. And they knew it wouldn't, because their mighty God was holding back the waters—a God they knew and trusted. Were these guys anxious as they stood there? Maybe glancing upstream now and then to see if a wall of water might be descending? I don't think they were fearful at all. I think they were marveling at the greatness of their God. That's why they could stand in harm's way. Their lives were in His hand. And so is yours.

Imagine for a minute what it would have been like to have been there.

(In some ways, I think I'd rather see this one than the Red Sea crossing.) These people had lived through hard and difficult years in the wilderness. And now, before they stepped one foot into that longed-for Promised Land, they got to experience the power of God firsthand—in a big, big way.

That's the thing about hardship. It puts iron in a man's soul. During the early days of the American Revolution, John and Abigail Adams carried on their close relationship by writing letters to one another. Although separated sometimes for years at a time, their hearts were joined together over the miles. On one occasion, Abigail wrote these words to her tired and fatigued husband:

> These are times in which a genius would wish to live. It is not in the still calm of life, or the repose of a pacific station, that great characters are formed.... The Habits of a vigorous mind are formed in contending with difficulties. All History will convince you of this, and that wisdom and penetration are the fruits of experience, not the Lessons of retirement and leisure. Great necessities call out great virtues. When a mind is raised, and animated by scenes that engage the Heart, then those qualities which would otherwise lay dormant, wake into Life, and form the Character of the Hero and the Statesman.[6]

What a dose of encouragement from a wife to a husband who was putting his life on the line for his family, his country—and the future of both.

5. He commanded the stones to be stacked—so the kids would honor His name.

Do you remember the new twelve-man team that Joshua was commanded to choose? Well, we left them sitting on the sidelines a few pages back. So why were they chosen and what was their task? It's all outlined for us in Joshua 4:

> When all the nation had finished passing over the Jordan, the LORD said to Joshua, "Take twelve men from the people, from each tribe a man, and command them, saying, 'Take twelve stones from here out of the midst of the Jordan, from the very place where the priests' feet stood firmly, and bring them over with you and lay them down in the place where you lodge tonight.'" Then Joshua called the twelve men from the people of Israel, whom he had appointed, a man from each tribe. And Joshua said to them, "Pass on before the ark of the LORD your God into the midst of the Jordan, and take up each of you a stone upon his shoulder, according to the number of the tribes of the people of Israel, that this may be a sign among you. When your children ask in time to come, 'What do those stones mean to you?' then you shall tell them that the waters of the Jordan were cut off before the ark of the covenant of the LORD. When it passed over the Jordan, the waters of the Jordan were cut off. So these stones shall be to the people of Israel a memorial forever."
>
> And the people of Israel did just as Joshua commanded and took up twelve stones out of the midst of the Jordan, according to the number of the tribes of the people of Israel, just as the LORD told Joshua. And they carried them over with them to the place where they lodged and laid them down there. And Joshua set up twelve stones in the midst of the Jordan, in the place where the feet of the priests bearing the ark of the covenant had stood; and they

are there to this day. For the priests bearing the ark stood in the midst of the Jordan until everything was finished that the LORD commanded Joshua to tell the people, according to all that Moses had commanded Joshua.

The people passed over in haste. And when all the people had finished passing over, the ark of the LORD and the priests passed over before the people. The sons of Reuben and the sons of Gad and the half-tribe of Manasseh passed over armed before the people of Israel, as Moses had told them. About 40,000 ready for war passed over before the LORD for battle, to the plains of Jericho. On that day the LORD exalted Joshua in the sight of all Israel, and they stood in awe of him just as they had stood in awe of Moses, all the days of his life.

And the LORD said to Joshua, "Command the priests bearing the ark of the testimony to come up out of the Jordan." So Joshua commanded the priests, "Come up out of the Jordan." And when the priests bearing the ark of the covenant of the LORD came up from the midst of the Jordan, and the soles of the priests' feet were lifted up on dry ground, the waters of the Jordan returned to their place and overflowed all its banks, as before.

The people came up out of the Jordan on the tenth day of the first month, and they encamped at Gilgal on the east border of Jericho. And those twelve stones, which they took out of the Jordan, Joshua set up at Gilgal. And he said to the people of Israel, "When your children ask their fathers in times to come, 'What do these stones mean?' then you shall let your children know, 'Israel passed over this Jordan on dry ground.' For the LORD

your God dried up the waters of the Jordan for you until
you passed over, as the LORD your God did to the Red
Sea, which he dried up for us until we passed over, so
that all the peoples of the earth may know that the hand
of the LORD is mighty, that you may fear the LORD your
God forever."

The twelve men were given a unique assignment. They were to make
two different stacks of twelve stones. After everyone had crossed on dry
land, they were to go out to the middle of the Jordan where the priests were
standing with the ark, and each man was to grab a good-sized stone, heft it
to his shoulder, and bring it over to where the people were. Then they were
commanded to go out a second time to the middle of the Jordan and do the
drill again. Only this time they made the stack of twelve stones right there
in the middle of the riverbed.

So now there are two piles of twelve stones—one on the bank and one
in the middle of the river. Now let me remind you that each time they went
out to the middle of the river they were putting themselves in harm's way.
Somewhere upstream, a *mountain* of water had been piling up. The priests
had been in harm's way the entire time, but now the twelve men were to
join them in their precarious position. They went out in faith, trusting that
God would continue to hold the water back. If He didn't, their corpses
would be washed thirty miles downstream. Once again, they were commanded to control their fear and do what God commanded. That's the
Christian life.

This was all done for one reason. They stacked the stones so that their
kids would one day come home for dinner and say, "Hey, Dad, what's the
deal with that pile of stones?" And then the father was to tell them the
story of what God had done. And as he told the story, God's name was
honored.

Twelve Stones

About eleven years ago we decided to look for a place on a couple of acres that would get us closer to our church. Our kids had become actively involved in the college and high school ministries, and the church was close to a fifty-minute drive away. It seemed like we were all making the drive two or three times a week.

We started looking around to see if we could find something closer to the church. After all, gas was getting up to $1.25 a gallon and that was just unbelievable. We looked around for a good six months, and just couldn't seem to come up with anything.

One day I was driving around in an area, trying to see what was available. As I looked around, I suddenly had the inspiration to drive by the Hickerson place. They had a little ranch—sort of a retreat center, actually—and the young couple that would keep our kids when we went out of town lived on their property in a little barn that had been converted into a house. Lamar and Jennifer had just moved out of state, and I needed to get their phone number. So I decided to swing by the Hickersons' and see if anyone was home who could give me the new number.

At that time, this place was quite a ways out in the country—although it was much closer to the church. So I pulled into the long driveway and drove down the little hill, hoping someone would be home. I knocked and Candy came to the door. I told her that I was trying to contact Lamar, and asked for his number. She invited me in and I waited by the front door as she went to get the number. When she found it and handed it to me, she asked, "So, Steve, what brings you all the way out here?"

"Oh, I'm just driving around the area looking for property."

And immediately she looked at me very strangely—almost as though she was shocked at what I said. I couldn't figure out what had happened. Had I said something inappropriate? Hadn't I simply told her I was out looking for property? But to see her face, you would have thought I'd told her North Korea had launched missiles that would hit Texas in the next ninety seconds. I'm not kidding. She seemed stunned by my words, and I couldn't figure out why.

Slowly, she repeated them: "You're out looking for property."

Trying to keep it casual, I replied that we were thinking about getting closer to the church, and that's why I was looking around.

"You ought to buy this place," she said.

And I laughed out loud. Literally I laughed.

"Excuse me for laughing," I quickly said. "I didn't mean to be rude. But I didn't even know your place was for sale. I didn't see a sign out front."

"We would never put a sign out front. You see, our daughter just got married and we have been praying for three years about selling once she was married. And we've decided to sell. We're going to move and build a much larger retreat center. But the Lord gave us this place twenty years ago, and we've raised our family here. We would never just sell to anyone off the street. We've been praying for three years that the Lord would bring along the right people that He has chosen for this property."

"Well, that's great. I'm sure He'll bring along the right family at the right time."

"Maybe it's you, Steve."

"It's not me, I can tell you that for sure."

"Well, how do you know that?"

"For starters, how much property do you have here? And how many houses?"

"Well, of course there's the main house, and then the little converted barn where Lamar and Jennifer were living, as well the little redwood cottage. And it's all situated on twenty acres."

"Well, I can assure you that I'm not even in the ball game on this. As a matter of fact, I'm not even in the parking lot."

"How do you know that?"

"Well, I know that one to two acres is the extent of my price range."

"Steve, you don't understand. *We're not looking for the right price, we're looking for the right family.*"

"That's a very gracious approach, and I'm sure the right family will show up before long. But I can assure you that it's not us."

For the next thirty minutes, she tried to convince me to at least be open to the possibility. Now I should tell you that I really didn't know this woman very well. We had met briefly on a couple of occasions. But she kept trying to persuade me that it was indeed possible.

The Hickersons had always used their property for ministry. Each building is very rustic and the setting is really unique. The property sits in a little valley bordered by a small creek. It's really hidden away, and therefore a perfect retreat setting. And nearly every weekend of the year, the property was used for various church small groups and individual study and prayer retreats. Missionaries home on furlough were welcome to stay on at no charge. That's how the property had always been used. It had been dedicated to the Lord twenty years before. And now they were praying for a family that would continue that ministry emphasis.

It took me thirty minutes to graciously pull myself away from the front door. I kept trying to open that door and make my exit but just as I would put my hand on the doorknob, Candy would have another reason why I should buy the property. She mentioned a price that was well below market value—way below. But the whole thing was nuts. What would we ever do with a property that size? We had just a regular house on a regular lot and it was all I could do to keep the grass cut.

The whole thing was so crazy that I didn't even mention it to Mary. But several days later, as I was watching Mary and Rachel cleaning up after dinner (I'm such a servant-leader), I said, "You know, I went by the Hickersons' a few days ago to get Lamar's phone number, and the funniest thing happened." I proceeded to tell Mary and Rachel about my conversation with Candy at the front door. They both knew the property well because they had been there several times. After I finished relating the strange details of our discussion at the front door, Mary looked at me and said, "I wonder if the Lord is in this?"

"No," I replied, "He's not. What would we do with a property that big? First of all, we couldn't afford it, and secondly, what would we *do* with it?"

Later that night my mom called from California. In the midst of our conversation, she asked me if I had found any property. I told her no, but then I mentioned the crazy conversation at the Hickerson place. I told her about Candy and how persistent she had been. When I completed the story, there was silence on the other end of the phone. And then my mom said, "Steve, I wonder if the Lord is in this."

"No, Mom, He's *not* in this. It's too crazy. What would we do with a property like that? And besides, I couldn't afford it."

"How do you know you can't afford it? That's an unbelievably low price. Have you done any homework on it?"

"Well ... no."

Later that night I went online to one of those mortgage calculators. I ran all the numbers and was shocked to find out that I did qualify. And we could handle the payments. But I still thought it was crazy.

A few days later Mary suggested that I talk with several of my close friends and run it by them. I smiled to myself, and thought, *Now that's a good idea because these guys are all very conservative financially, and they will immediately advise against it.*

A couple of days later I ran it by the first guy. I have a tremendous respect for his walk with the Lord—and he is an extremely good business mind. I told him the story and gave him the details on the property. He listened carefully and then surprised me with his answer. "Steve," he said, "I wouldn't dismiss this too quickly. *I wonder if the Lord might be in this.*"

I had talked with three people about this, and each of them said, "I wonder if the Lord might be in this." I was starting to get a little nervous. This really wasn't something I wanted to pursue. It made no sense to me. What in the world would we do with a small retreat center?

So the next week, my friend Gary Rosberg was in town. I told him the story, adding my analysis that the whole thing was nuts.

"Can you show me the place?" he asked.

That kind of surprised me. I called and asked if we could drive by, and Candy said sure. So we walked around the property for about a half hour, and then Gary suddenly stopped and looked at me. "Steve, can you give me one good reason why you wouldn't move ahead on this?"

I was stunned. This did *not* fit my long-term plan. We had a normal house on a normal lot and I was within a year of having that normal house paid off. I wasn't looking for a bigger property—let alone a retreat center. I just wanted to speak, write my books, and hang out with Mary and the kids on a couple of acres. I didn't need to be Ben Cartwright on the Ponderosa (you young guys will have to Google that to understand).

So what was God doing? I wanted two acres and now I found myself looking at twenty. And the people I respected most were encouraging me to move ahead.

I talked with seven more people. People I had known for a long time, people who knew me and my family, and had a consistent walk with the Lord. One of them was a real estate attorney I just "happened" to sit next to on a plane in California. We hadn't seen each other in five or six years. Before the trip was over, I had told him my story and the details. As we were landing at John Wayne Airport in Orange County, he looked at me and said, "Steve, I don't see any red flags at all. Perhaps the Lord is in this."

This was getting ridiculous. We decided to put our house up for sale. It wasn't the greatest market, but we got two full-price offers in a matter of days.

Long story short—we bought the place.

A few days before closing, we were having dinner with the Hickersons and Candy said, "Steve, I think I need to explain to you my unusual behavior that day you came by the house and we had our conversation by the front door.

"As you know, we had been praying about making this move for three years. We decided to definitely hold off until our daughter got married and moved out. But once that happened, the reality of leaving the home where we had raised our kids really began to hit me. I had a lot of memories wrapped up in that place. I truly believed that the Lord wanted us to take the next step and build the larger retreat center, but I was having a tough time with the thought of leaving. I needed to confirm everything in my heart, so I took a day just to pray and wait on the Lord.

"I asked Him to make it crystal clear to us if this was His leading. I wanted to be obedient—but I needed to know for sure. And toward the end of the day, I prayed that the Lord would strengthen my faith because I was struggling. I asked Him to do something pretty unusual. I prayed and asked the Lord that whoever it was that He had chosen to buy our property, that He would bring them to the front door and they would tell me that they were looking for property. We were so far off the beaten path that I figured that would be a very strong confirmation. Seven days later you knocked on the front door and within two minutes told me that you were out looking for property. That's why I was so persuasive and talkative. I *knew* you and Mary were the ones."

I couldn't believe it. What a story. We've been here eleven years now. And over the years this place has not only been a personal retreat for when I come home from speaking, but it's been a place for young people to stay as they complete college, nursing programs, and seminary degrees. It's been a place where families have stayed who were in need of housing and where prayer groups have been able to get away and meet with the Lord. And we have never charged anyone a dime to stay here—whether it's for a weekend or three years. The rental income would be nice, but from day one we knew God was giving this to us as a refuge, and we should do the same for anyone else that He sent our way. So it's been our privilege to do that, and a great deal of ministry has taken place—ministry of the sort I could have never imagined.

A few months after we moved in, we took twelve good-sized stones from down by the creek and we piled them up front by the gate. A friend carved out a little wooden sign. It simply says, "Twelve Stones Ranch."

And when people ask, "What's the pile of stones all about?" I just tell them the story. *And God's name is honored.*

It's the manly thing to do.

Chapter Ten

Three Tasks

"What should government do? As little as possible."
—Paul Johnson

Paul Johnson is a world-class historian and a former advisor to Prime Minister Margaret Thatcher of Great Britain. Johnson once told Mrs. Thatcher: "There are three things a government must handle, for no one else can: external defense, internal order and maintaining an honest currency." Mrs. Thatcher was so impressed by this simple observation that she reached into her large purse, pulled out a pen and a notebook, and wrote it down.[1]

For a government it's three things:

- External defense
- Internal order
- Honest currency

When you're speaking about the governments of men, that simple analysis is about as concise and on target as it gets. You can add all the bells and whistles you please, but those three elements are the irreducible minimum of any viable government.

There are also three essential elements that pertain to the kingdom of God.

I find these elements rising out of three significant events occurring in quick succession after Israel's miraculous crossing of the Jordan. These three events yield three lessons to those who say to the Lord (and really mean it), "Use me!" In other words, to be used by God requires three consistent actions:

- Take the mark.
- Trust His provision.
- Take a knee.

I find no exceptions to these principles. Just as they became critical truths for Joshua and the great nation he led, so they are critical to us today, and the lives that we lead in our contemporary world. All three of these events are recorded in Joshua 5. Let's hit them one by one.

1. Take the mark.

This first principle derives from an extremely painful experience that every male in Israel had to endure after crossing the Jordan and setting foot in the land of promise.

Every man was circumcised.

Yes, you read that correctly. Joshua 5:1–9 records the specific (and painful) details:

> As soon as all the kings of the Amorites who were beyond the Jordan to the west, and all the kings of the Canaanites who were by the sea, heard that the LORD had dried up the waters of the Jordan for the people of Israel until they had crossed over, their hearts melted and there was no longer any spirit in them because of the people of Israel.

At that time the LORD said to Joshua, "Make flint knives and circumcise the sons of Israel a second time." So Joshua made flint knives and circumcised the sons of Israel at Gibeath-haaraloth. And this is the reason why Joshua circumcised them: all the males of the people who came out of Egypt, all the men of war, had died in the wilderness on the way after they had come out of Egypt. Though all the people who came out had been circumcised, yet all the people who were born on the way in the wilderness after they had come out of Egypt had not been circumcised. For the people of Israel walked forty years in the wilderness, until all the nation, the men of war who came out of Egypt, perished, because they did not obey the voice of the LORD; the LORD swore to them that he would not let them see the land that the LORD had sworn to their fathers to give to us, a land flowing with milk and honey. So it was their children, whom he raised up in their place, that Joshua circumcised. For they were uncircumcised, because they had not been circumcised on the way.

When the circumcising of the whole nation was finished, they remained in their places in the camp until they were healed. And the LORD said to Joshua, "Today I have rolled away the reproach of Egypt from you." And so the name of that place is called Gilgal to this day.

I found it somewhat uncomfortable just to read that account. So what does this mean? How do we apply this?

Well, I don't think you apply it by getting it done yourself; I don't think that's what the Lord is speaking to us about in this passage. (Do I hear a sigh of relief?)

It's important how you interpret the Bible, and this is one of those issues where you really want to make sure you're doing it right. So don't call a doctor for the circumcision, and don't try this at home—with a flint knife or anything else.

I say these things, perhaps, because I'm reminded of the story of Origen (Origenes Adamantius, AD 185–254), a powerful teacher in the early Christian church. In fact, some of Origen's works are read to this very day.

He was a godly guy, this Origen, but he wasn't perfect by any means. Even a great scholar of his stature could get some Bible passages wrong. For instance, when he read Matthew 19:12, he concluded that it was speaking to him and that he should become a eunuch for the kingdom of God.[2] So he went home and castrated himself. Once again, it's very important to interpret the Scripture correctly. Otherwise it can be very painful—not to mention sending your voice an octave or two higher.

So what is this circumcision thing that all the men in Israel had to do after they crossed the Jordan River? What does this really mean?

Let's bottom-line what happened. When the nation was wandering in the wilderness for forty years because of the unbelief of the ten spies, none of the Israeli males were circumcised. "Circumcision is the surgical removal of the foreskin of the male sexual organ. Circumcision was widely practiced in the ancient world, including the Egyptian and Canaanite cultures. But among these people the rite was performed at the beginning of puberty, or about twelve years of age, for hygienic reasons or as a sort of initiation ceremony into manhood. In contrast, the Hebrew people performed circumcision on infants."[3]

The male infants were circumcised on the eighth day after their birth. This was commanded by God in the covenant that He made with Abraham (Gen. 17:9–14). The proof that God had made a covenant to bless Abraham and His people was not written on a piece of paper, it was marked on the sexual organ of every male in Israel.

But when they were wandering in the wilderness, circumcision wasn't practiced by the people. As a result, it had to be taken care of before the fighting men went to war against all the *-ites* of Canaan. God required it of His men at that time, and when you're counting on God to help you tackle the giants, you want to make sure that you've been obedient to Him—in every detail.

So all the men under the age of forty had to take the mark before they attempted to take the land promised to them in the covenant with Abraham. They could not go into battle unless they had the promise of the covenant upon their own bodies.

Now interestingly enough, it was the worst possible time to take the mark. (We seem to keep running into that concept, don't we?)

Thousands and thousands of men in Israel were suddenly on the injured reserve list. When an adult male has his foreskin cut, he is what you call "out of action." This isn't the kind of deal where you take a couple of Tylenol and feel better in the morning. It's important that we see the historical situation here. This is not some fantasy tale. This really happened.

In this situation, by being obedient to the commandment of God, they were facing *the giant of complete vulnerability*. They had absolutely no ability to mount their own defense. If the Lord didn't protect them while they were incapacitated, they would be slaughtered.[4]

Every one of them understood all too well that for several days they would be completely dependent upon God to defend their lives. From their very hearts, they had to trust in God to protect and defend them from their enemies.

And that leads us to the second idea of circumcision. Circumcision was more than a physical issue; it was to be spiritual as well. Not only were their sexual organs to be circumcised, but their hearts were to be circumcised too.

Deuteronomy 10:16 declares, "Circumcise therefore the foreskin of your heart, and be no longer stubborn." In Jeremiah 4:4, God says, "Circumcise yourselves to the LORD; remove the foreskin of your hearts."

This wasn't just an external sign—it was to be inside their hearts as well. When they took the mark on their sexual organs, their hearts had to be marked too. Otherwise, they wouldn't have had the faith to trust in God's protection and defense.

So why did God insist on circumcision for every man in Israel?

> The act of circumcision itself symbolized a complete separation from the widely prevalent sins of the flesh: adultery, fornication, and sodomy. Further, the rite had spiritual overtones not only in relation to sexual conduct but in every phase of life.... So Israel was to understand that circumcision was not simply a cutting of flesh; also their lives were to be holy.[5]

We are saved by sheer grace and by trusting in the Lord Jesus Christ alone. But once He regenerates us and gives us eternal life—He now wants us to live lives that are pleasing to Him. Our salvation is utterly from Him—He is the One who justifies us forever. But we are also now to live out His life in our lives. He desires to change us from babes into men. So after we are saved, baptism is an important first step in following Him. But it only reflects on the outside what has already taken place inside in our hearts and souls.

Every Jewish male was circumcised physically. But if a guy wasn't circumcised in heart, it was only a religious observance.

They had taken the mark in their hearts.

When you take the mark, it affects:

- Your thinking
- Your looking
- Your speaking

- Your touching/handling
- Your walking

The heart is not only central to our sexual behaviors, it is critical to walking by faith. Everything within Christianity is an issue of the heart. It's always about the heart. It was about the heart in Old Testament: "You shall love the LORD your God with all your heart and with all your soul and with all your might" (Deut. 6:5). And it's about the heart in the New Testament as well. Note the emphasis on the heart out of just five verses in Romans 10:

> But the righteousness based on faith says, "Do not say in your heart, 'Who will ascend into heaven?'" (that is, to bring Christ down) or "'Who will descend into the abyss?'" (that is, to bring Christ up from the dead). But what does it say? "The word is near you, in your mouth and in your heart" (that is, the word of faith that we proclaim); because, if you confess with your mouth that Jesus is Lord and believe in your heart that God raised him from the dead, you will be saved. For with the heart one believes and is justified, and with the mouth one confesses and is saved. (vv. 6–10)

So the heart is everything. And in the Scriptures, the heart represents not that thing beating in your chest, but the essence of everything that you are. The "heart" encompasses your mind, will, and emotions. That's why we will say to someone, "Put your heart into it!" What does that mean? It means to put everything about you into something.

The Dallas Cowboys currently have a running back by the name of Marion Barber. If you've ever seen number 24 take a handoff, you know why I bring him up. On every single play, Marion Barber puts his heart into it. When he takes that handoff, he only has one speed—*all out*. Barber gives it all he's got on every play. He takes on tacklers head-on and punishes them. It usually takes two or three guys to take Barber down—and that's after he's leveled two or three other guys. In his third year with the Cowboys, even though Barber was the second-string running back, he was named to the Pro Bowl by the other players in the league. They know when a guy is putting his heart into it.

Now watch how this works. We all, at one time or another, have to face the giant of complete vulnerability. We are absolutely defenseless in a particular situation. It may be a performance review at work or a situation where your character and reputation are being assaulted.

It might be a physical disease to which we are completely vulnerable. It could a hundred different situations—but the point is that you are completely vulnerable. The men of Israel on the west side of the Jordan were vulnerable because they had been circumcised. A thirty-eight-year-old guy who has been circumcised the day before isn't going to be much help if a marauding army shows up. So this is where the circumcision of the heart is critical. Those guys who have taken the mark on their hearts are going to be demonstrating their faith by putting their complete trust in God to see them through and deliver them. That's how they face and conquer the giant of complete vulnerability. It's an issue from the heart.

When the Lord told Joshua to circumcise all the men in that situation, I'm sure that Joshua experienced some immediate fear. What the Lord was telling him to do went cross-grain to common sense!

Mark this and underline it: Joshua didn't let his fear or inadequacy keep him from moving ahead. He didn't allow the fear to paralyze or stop him. He kept moving in the right direction—he kept following the Lord—he kept serving the Lord. He was obedient because he was obedient from the *heart*.

So what do you do with those fears and inadequacies that burden you and weigh you down? Well, you throw them on the Lord and you keep moving. Or in their case, they kept recovering because they couldn't move.

That's the clear instruction in Psalm 55:22 (NASB): "Cast your burden upon the LORD and He will sustain you." The margin in the New American Standard Bible offers an alternative reading of the original language. Check this out—"Cast what He has given you upon the LORD and He will sustain you."

Now what does that mean? Just this: The situations that frighten us and overwhelm us are actually scenarios from the Lord designed to test our faith and strengthen our faith. It was Thomas Watson who declared, "Whatever the affliction, it is the Lord who sends it."

So how do you handle these fears and burdens? You cast what He has given you right back on Him. If He didn't want you in this particular situation, you wouldn't be there. Perhaps you are completely vulnerable to a potential devastating force. And there is nothing that you can do.

Cast it on Him. After all, He's the One who has allowed you to be where you find yourself. And as you cast it on Him, knowing that He will somehow bring good out of your difficult and disastrous situation, you will find that He will sustain you.

The men of Israel were utterly helpless as they recovered from circumcision. It would be days before they would be well enough to stand up and defend their families. As they were recovering, their greatest enemy was the anxiety of what might happen. What if an army shows up this afternoon? Or maybe not this afternoon, but in the morning? This was the battle they were facing. They had to fight off anxious thoughts of fear and worry while they were completely vulnerable. They had to take those fears and worries and cast them on the Lord.

We face at times the same anxieties when we are completely vulnerable. So what do we do? We have taken the mark, but we must do battle against wrong thoughts. Martyn Lloyd-Jones (yes, I know, this is the third time I've quoted him) supplies such great wisdom when he says, "A large part of faith, especially in this connection, consists of just refusing anxious thoughts. That to me is perhaps the most important and the most practical thing of all. Faith means refusing to think about worrying things, refusing to think of the future in that wrong sense. The devil and all adverse circumstances will do their utmost to make me do so, but having faith means that I shall say, 'No; I refuse to be worried. I have done my reasonable service; I have done what I believed to be right and legitimate, and beyond that I will not think at all.' That is faith, and it is particularly true with regard to the future…. Faith is refusing to be burdened because we have cast our burden upon the Lord."[6]

2. Trust His provision.

The next event immediately after the circumcision is huge—but it could easily be missed by a quick reading. Here's the text of Joshua 5:10–12. See if you can pick up the critical detail:

> While the people of Israel were encamped at Gilgal, they
> kept the Passover on the fourteenth day of the month in
> the evening on the plains of Jericho. And the day after the
> Passover, on that very day, they ate of the produce of the
> land, unleavened cakes and parched grain. And the manna
> ceased the day after they ate of the produce of the land.
> And there was no longer manna for the people of Israel,
> but they ate of the fruit of the land of Canaan that year.

The key detail is found in the phrase "and the manna ceased." For forty years, God fed these two million men, women, and children. That's a lot of chow. Can you imagine the supply line it would take to feed two million people every day for forty years? That would be a monumental problem for us, but is anything too hard for the Lord? Of course not.

God didn't provide them anything that they were familiar with. He didn't give them cheeseburgers and He didn't give them tacos. He gave them *manna*. When they first saw it, they had no idea what it was. They had never seen anything like it before. All of the details about the manna are described in Exodus 16:13–36.

In the morning the manna showed up with the morning dew. It was like a honey wafer with coriander seeds. Apparently, it was the original protein bar. It was very versatile, in that it could be baked or boiled. In the morning they would pick up enough for each family member for that day. If they took too much or if they took too little, it came exactly to the right measurement, which was an "omer." In other words, if they were to take a pound for each adult, and one woman picked up three quarters of a pound and another woman picked up a pound and a quarter, God made sure that in each case it came exactly to a pound. They were not to pick up any more than they needed for that day. Each person was to eat their complete portion before going to bed. Nothing was to be left, because if it was, it would immediately turn to worms.

And the next morning, the fresh manna would be there for that day. On the sixth day, they were to pick up enough manna for two days since they weren't given manna on the Sabbath. But when they picked up a two-day supply, the manna for the second day didn't go bad. God supernaturally watched over the entire process, and that's how He fed them for forty years.

In the Lord's Prayer, recorded in Matthew 6, Jesus said that we are to ask God to provide our daily bread. This is what the manna was. It was their daily bread for forty years. And they ate of it until they crossed the Jordan, the men were circumcised, they observed the Passover, and had access to food in the Promised Land.

There is a giant that every man dreads facing. It is *the giant of financial drought.* Before irrigation, the greatest threat to a farmer was drought. There is a classic old painting that I have seen several times. I don't know the name of the artist, but the painting itself is very clear in my mind. In the midst of a newly furrowed field is a husband and wife. I would imagine from their dress and look that it portrays a scene from the 1920s or 30s. The husband has obviously just planted his seed. He is kneeling in the field with his hat off and his head bowed. His wife is standing to his side and slightly behind him. Her head is bowed and her hand is on his shoulder. The picture is quite obvious in its message. They are asking God to send the rain upon the newly planted seed. They are completely dependent upon God for His provision.

Back in the Depression days of the thirties, when families sat down to a meal and first gave thanks to God for His provision, they *meant* it. They were thankful for their daily bread. It was a gift from God's good hand.

We often hear of families who live paycheck to paycheck. But how about living *day to day?* Nobody wants to be in that position. Everybody wants plenty of money in the bank and as much financial security as possible.

Everyone except George Müller. As we noted in an earlier chapter, George Müller was a unique man and a man of great faith. Even though we've already met him in the pages of this book, it would be worthwhile to circle the plane and take another look at the big picture of this amazing life.

Müller is famous for the orphanages he established in Bristol, England, back in 1836. He started with thirty orphans and by 1879 the five orphan houses were caring for, educating, and teaching two thousand orphans each day. Over a period of sixty-three years, Müller cared for more than one hundred twenty thousand orphans.[7]

I know what it is to raise three kids.

Can you imagine one hundred twenty thousand?

Can you imagine the financial pressure, and the amount of funds that it would take to feed, clothe, and teach these children? Müller started his orphanage with a radical purpose and mission. He wanted to demonstrate to people that God was the *living God* who would meet the daily needs of His people. He began the orphanage with the thought that he would only share his needs with God; he would not ask anyone to give money to the work of the orphanage, or make their needs known. It is a phenomenal book to read when you feel like you need your faith stretched a bit (and who doesn't feel that?).

My copy of his autobiography runs 736 pages. In the pages of that book, Müller included meticulous daily records of the financial needs of the orphanage—and the miraculous financial provision that God brought in on daily basis. It really is a record of how God, for sixty-seven years, brought in the manna that the orphans needed to survive.

I must emphasize again that Müller started his orphanage with the stated purpose that he would trust God through prayer to meet their needs. Müller claimed from his detailed records that over thirty thousand of his prayer requests were answered in the same hour or on the same day that he made them to the Lord.

Müller aimed many of his meditations at Christians who wrestle with various financial difficulties. The Lord used such struggles in his own life, he admitted, to …

> awaken in my heart the desire of setting before the church at large, and before the world, a proof that He has not in the least changed; and this seemed to me best done by the establishing of an orphan house. It needed to be something that could be seen, even by the natural eye. Now, if I, a poor man, simply by prayer and faith, obtained, without asking any individual, the means for establishing and carrying on an orphan house, there would be something which, with the Lord's blessing, might be instrumental in

strengthening the faith of the children of God, besides
being a testimony to the consciences of the unconverted
of the reality of the things of God.[8]

If you desire to be used by God, you will more than likely have to face
the giant of financial drought. Financial drought occurs when your steady,
reliable source of income dries up. As drought stops the rain, so financial
drought stops your source of cash flow.

In case you've never experienced this, let me give you a tip: This is a
stressful occurrence. But when God stops a financial source that has always
been there, it simply means that He is going to open another source that
you know nothing about.

Under Joshua's leadership, the people have crossed the Jordan and
entered the land. They have observed the Passover. And now, the day after
the Passover observance, God says to Joshua, "I'm pulling the manna.
Starting tomorrow you will eat off the land." So suddenly, after forty years,
God dries up their source of food. But now they are surrounded by fields of
grain that they can harvest to feed their families.

There it is. Do you see the principle?

*When God dries up your secure and familiar source, He will provide
another.* And He works the timing so that not even one day's provision is
missed.

God is our provider. One of His names is Jehovah-Jireh, which means
"the Lord will provide." On one particular day, George Müller needed funds
to feed the orphans and make some needed repairs on his buildings. A man
came by and gave him a magnificent diamond ring. In response, Müller did
something very unusual. He used the magnificent diamond to scratch on
his office windowpane the words "Jehovah-Jireh."

There is a great statement from the Lord in Isaiah 46:3–4 (NASB):

Listen to Me, O house of Jacob,
   And all the remnant of the house of Israel,
   You who have been borne by Me from birth
   And have been carried from the womb;
Even to your old age I will be the same,
   And even to your graying years I will bear you!
   I have done it, and I will carry you;
   And I will bear you and I will deliver you.

There's your promise to fight off the giant of financial drought. In the opening statement of his autobiography, Müller states that he is specifically writing for those who carry great fears of future financial drought. Is that you? Do you wonder how you will get your kids through college and save enough for retirement? Do you wonder how you will recover from a staggering financial loss? The answer is in Isaiah 46. God promises to carry you. He has formed you in the womb, He has birthed you, He has carried you all of your life, and He will continue to carry you, until the day you check out of the Earth Hotel and enter the (real) Promised Land.

Your current source of income may dry up. But if it does, God will simply bring it another way. That's the promise. You can live off that today.

3. Take a knee.

Let's quickly update the situation.

The men are healed up and the Passover meal has been celebrated. The Passover was the meal they would eat to remember the night when the angel of death passed over the homes that had the blood on the doorpost. But for the homes of the Egyptians that did not have blood over the door, every firstborn child was killed. The angel of death passed over all the families of Israel because they were under the blood.

After this great celebration and remembrance, Joshua got off by himself for a while, looking into the distance at the massive fortress of a city named Jericho. And as he did so, a life-changing encounter took place.

The new mantle of leadership must have been weighing rather heavily on Joshua's shoulders. He was the leader of Israel and the general of her army. The buck stopped with him. And as he perused from afar the massive walls of Jericho, a warrior suddenly appeared out of nowhere.

> When Joshua was by Jericho, he lifted up his eyes and looked, and behold, a man was standing before him with his drawn sword in his hand. And Joshua went to him and said to him, "Are you for us, or for our adversaries?" And he said, "No; but I am the commander of the army of the LORD. Now I have come." And Joshua fell on his face to the earth and worshiped and said to him, "What does my lord say to his servant?" And the commander of the LORD's army said to Joshua, "Take off your sandals from your feet, for the place where you are standing is holy." And Joshua did so. (Josh. 5:13–15)

Whoever this man was, he was suddenly in the camp and he was holding a sword. Not surprisingly, Joshua immediately asked him to declare himself. And that's when it dawned on Joshua that he was standing in the presence of his Commander and Captain.

It's not uncommon after a football practice for a coach to say to the team, "Everybody gather around and take a knee."

In the Christian life, to take a knee means that you bow and that you obey. When Joshua realized he was in the presence of the Lord, he didn't take a knee—he took two knees and got on his face.

Here's the message of that encounter: He's the Captain—you're not. So get off the throne and acknowledge that He is on the throne. He's the King, the Master, the Lord, the Captain, and the Commander in Chief.

When God called to Moses from the burning bush, Moses was told to take off the sandals from his feet because he was standing on holy ground (Ex. 3:5). Moses was in the presence of God.

At first, Joshua was unsure of who this man with the sword was. But when he understood that it was the captain of the Lord's army, he fell on his face. But then he was given the same instructions that Moses received: Take off your sandals; you are standing on holy ground. This captain, this commander, was God—a preincarnate appearance of the Lord Jesus Christ to Joshua. It was this great Commander who would go ahead of Joshua and the people and give them victory in the battles they were about to fight.

Later in his life, Joshua made his famous declaration before the people of Israel: "As for me and my house, we will serve the Lord" (Josh. 24:15). I believe that he made that same declaration in his heart as he bowed before the commander of the Lord's army.

I want to pull in here two insightful paragraphs from the pen of James Montgomery Boice. Dr. Boice, now at home with the Lord, was a tremendous student of the Word, and his words carry great truth:

> Joshua was a soldier. He was a brilliant soldier, one of the most extraordinary military commanders of all time. But he was not an exciting personality, as far as we can tell. He was probably just a bit of a plugger, a rather straightforward man who was chiefly concerned with carrying out his divine commission to the letter. He had no great sins and made very few mistakes. In short,

he was not the kind of person who would make a good hero for a novel. Yet Joshua was eminently God's man. God told him at the very beginning of the conquest: "Be careful to obey all the law my servant Moses gave you; do not turn from it to the right or left, that you may be successful wherever you go" (Joshua 1:7). This is exactly what Joshua did! And he was successful....

As I have studied Joshua, I have become convinced that this is a message very much needed in our time. We have many professing Christians in our day; as many as 50 million in the United States alone, by some estimates. But we do not seem to have many Joshuas. We do not have many who, without trying to be novel or spectacular, determine to obey the law of God in every particular and then actually do obey it throughout a lifetime of faithful service. Isn't it true that this is the chief reason for the church's weakness in our country at the present time? And isn't the chief reason for this failure our more basic failure to read, study, digest, and obey the word of God?[9]

Boice's diagnosis cuts right to the heart of matter.

We need some Joshuas. We don't need any more flashy leaders who are little more than Christian entertainers. We need some authentic leaders who are great submitters, who are under the authority of Christ and make it their life's ambition—beyond all else—to please Him. And they please Him by keeping His commandments.

We've got a lot of professing Christians. They can talk a good game. But we need some guys who are determined to live out their faith and follow Christ—no matter what, no matter where. Too many men today are rationalizing away their behavior. Too many men are playing the church game. But it's the rare man who just keeps following Christ day by day. He's not looking for the spotlight. He just wants to obey the orders he has received from the Captain and Commander.

As Louis L'Amour would say, that's a man to ride the river with. Or maybe a man to cross the Jordan with. That's a Joshua.

There is a giant that sometimes looks very attractive. And that is *the giant of half-hearted obedience.* When you serve the Lord, you obey the Lord. Joshua swore his absolute obedience to the Lord as he bowed before Him with the great city of Jericho in the background.

A soldier that disobeys orders from his superior officer will be punished severely. Yes, Joshua was the leader of Israel, but he himself was in absolute submission to the commands of a greater Captain. A man who obeys when he wants to, a man who obeys when it fits in with his agenda, should seriously ask if he really knows the Lord. Note the words of 1 John 2:4 (NASB): "The one who says, 'I have come to know Him,' and does not keep His commandments, is a liar, and the truth is not in him."

Those are strong words that hit us right in the mouth.

Do you know Him? Then you will desire in your heart of hearts to obey Him and please Him. Do you perfectly obey? No. You may *want* to, but you fall short and sin sometimes. Welcome to the club. The man who says he walks in perfect obedience 24-7 is also a liar. First John 1:8 declares that "if we say we have no sin, we deceive ourselves, and the truth is not in us." First John 1:10 repeats the principle: "If we say we have not sinned, we make him a liar, and his word is not in us."

Bottom line, true believers really want to practice the truth. In their heart of hearts, they genuinely desire to live it out, to grow stronger every day, and to apply the Word to their lives. But someone who isn't too worried about obedience and pleasing the Commander isn't going to give himself to practicing the truth. First John 1:6 states that "If we say we have fellowship with him while we walk in darkness, we lie and do not practice the truth."

So who are we? We are soldiers in the Lord's army, men who have sworn our total allegiance to Him … and men who also happen to be flawed. But the strong and continual desire in our heart of hearts is to be obedient, and to please our Commander. Some men have become such liars that they lie when they don't need to lie. In contrast, God's men fight lying in their own lives. They hate lying! They are constantly practicing the truth! And when they stumble, they immediately acknowledge it and straighten it out.

We don't have to live perfect lives of obedience to please Him. If you say that you are living a perfect life of obedience you are lying. So what's the solution?

The solution for those who desire to obey but disobey at times is found in 1 John 1:9 (NASB): "If we confess our sins, He is faithful and righteous to forgive us our sins and to cleanse us from all unrighteousness."

He is our Commander in Chief, and must own our total and complete allegiance. He commands, and we obey. In other words, He calls the shots. So let's quit messing around with sin. Do what He says—obey your orders!

In your gut you know that's right.

And in your heart, that's what you really want to do.

Chapter Eleven

Two Spies

"Two are better than one."
—*Ecclesiastes 4:9*

Do you remember the old spiritual "Joshua Fit the Battle of the Death Star"?

I believe the actual title was "Joshua Fit the Battle of Jericho."

Let me give you a heads-up on Jericho. Jericho was the Death Star of Joshua's day.

I'm not a big Star Wars fan. I just now had to look up the fact that there are now six movies in the Star Wars series. I've seen the original *Star Wars* and the original sequel, *The Empire Strikes Back*, and that was about all the Star Wars I needed. I haven't really kept up with George Lucas and all the subsequent sequels and prequels. It got a little too confusing when I realized that *Star Wars* (the first movie) somehow became episode four. Apparently I'm not the only one who got confused. This got so complicated that even Lucas couldn't keep up with it.

I actually remember the first movie very well. Mary and I saw it in Florida on our honeymoon. Do you remember the scene when you first caught a glimpse of the Death Star? At first it looked like a planet or maybe a moon. But as you drew closer to that monstrosity, you realized it wasn't a planet at all: It was a massive, formidable killing machine.

Now I'm going to actually quote the description of the Death Star from the Star Wars Web site, and I'm doing this to make a point. I know that you are interested in studying the life of Joshua and Caleb more than Luke Skywalker—but stay with me here. I'm going somewhere with this!

> The Death Star was the code name of an unspeakably powerful and horrific weapon developed by the Empire. The immense space station carried a weapon capable of destroying entire planets. The Death Star was to be an instrument of terror, meant to cow treasonous worlds with the threat of annihilation....
>
> The Death Star was a battle station the size of a small moon. It had a formidable array of turbolasers and tractor beam projectors, giving it the firepower of greater than half the Imperial starfleet. Within its cavernous interior were legions of Imperial troops and fightercraft, as well as all manner of detention blocks and interrogation cells. The Death Star was spherical, and dark gray in color. Located on the Death Star's northern hemisphere was a concave disk housing the station's main laser weapon.
>
> Scattered across the Death Star's surface were thousands of weapons emplacements: a total of 10,000 turbolaser batteries, 2,500 laser cannons, 2,500 ion cannons, and 768 tractor beam projectors. The station carried a crew of 265,675, plus 52,276 gunners, 607,360 troops, 25,984 stormtroopers, 42,782 ship support staff, and 167,216 pilots and support crew. The station also carried 7,200 starfighters, four strike cruisers, 3,600 assault shuttles, 1,400 AT-ATs, 1,400 AT-STs, 1,860 drop ships, and more.[1]

Here's the point: Jericho was the Canaanite equivalent of the Death Star. No, Jericho didn't have lasers. But it had massive walls, and it was a city that was built for war. It was designed to fight off any attacks, sieges, or weapons that were known to the armies of the world at that time. *It could not be breached.* "From a human standpoint, the conquest of Jericho was impossible."[2]

"The walls were of a type which made direct assault practically impossible. An approaching enemy first encountered a stone abutment, eleven feet high, back and up from which sloped a thirty-five-degree plastered scarp reaching to the main wall some thirty-five vertical feet above. The steep, smooth slope prohibited battering the wall by any effective device or building fires to break it. An army trying to storm the wall found difficulty in climbing the slope, and ladders to scale it could find no satisfactory footing."[3]

The city was built on a mound of about eight acres. "A massive six-foot-thick wall was erected on the edge of the mound. The inner wall was separated from it by a space of from twelve to fifteen feet, and was itself twelve feet thick.... The wall originally reached perhaps a height of about thirty feet.... The crowded conditions led to the erection of houses over the space between the inner and outer walls."[4]

Do you see why I referred to Jericho as the "Death Star"? It could not be penetrated or breached. The city was "tightly shut." It could not be pried open by Joshua or by any other military commander. So the Lord Himself gave Joshua specific instructions on what to do in Joshua 6:1–5:

> Now Jericho was shut up inside and outside because of
> the people of Israel. None went out, and none came in.
> And the LORD said to Joshua, "See, I have given Jericho
> into your hand, with its king and mighty men of valor.
> You shall march around the city, all the men of war going

around the city once. Thus shall you do for six days. Seven priests shall bear seven trumpets of rams' horns before the ark. On the seventh day you shall march around the city seven times, and the priests shall blow the trumpets. And when they make a long blast with the ram's horn, when you hear the sound of the trumpet, then all the people shall shout with a great shout, and the wall of the city will fall down flat, and the people shall go up, everyone straight before him."

The walls that could not be breached or burned or captured just simply collapsed. Joshua very carefully obeyed the exact orders he had been given by the Lord. And as a result, the Lord gave him a great victory over Jericho, the Old Testament Death Star.

But I want to rewind back to Joshua 2.

Brave and Bold

I believe the conquest of Jericho really began in the second chapter of Joshua, not the sixth. The fall of the mighty city had its genesis with two very bold men—and in this case, I *don't* mean Joshua and Caleb. I'm referring to two other men who made the initial foray into Jericho in order to bring back an intelligence report to Joshua. Their names were—well, actually we don't know their names, because they are never mentioned in the text. They're just two of many faithful and courageous people in the pages of Scripture who served God with all their hearts, but remain nameless.

In the end, all that really matters is that God knows their names. And we can learn from these bold men whether we know their names or not.

When I get to heaven, however, I want to shake their hands and honor them by name.

Joshua has just been given a commission from the Lord as the new leader of the nation of Israel. Upon receiving his leadership post, the very first thing he does is to pick another group of spies to do another recon mission. This time the target of the mission will be Jericho, the great Death Star of the Canaanites.

And on this mission he doesn't pick twelve men; he chooses two.

Why just two? Why not one?

Solomon kicks in here and gives us the probable cause for Joshua's selection of two men instead of one. In Ecclesiastes 4:9 (NASB), we read, "Two are better than one because they have a good return for their labor." Two men working on a job are more productive and more profitable than one guy doing it by himself.

One of the giants that can quickly bring a man down is *the giant of going it alone.* When God made Adam, He made the pronouncement "It is not good for the man to be alone" (Gen. 2:18 NASB). So the Lord made a helper for him. By the way, a "helper" is not a term of weakness or lesser value. In Scripture, this very term is used of God Himself. He is our helper! We have been given a task and we can't pull it off by ourselves. One draft horse can pull a lot of weight—but two draft horses teamed up together can pull three to four times the weight that just one of them can.

There is another reason why two are stronger than one. One of the enemy's greatest weapons against a man who desires to be used for God's glory is discouragement.

Most of us aren't involved in "big" things, like doing recon of Jericho or taking out an Iranian nuclear lab. Most of our lives, we find ourselves doing "average" things or "small" things, and we begin to get discouraged because we look at our lives and don't see anything that seems really significant (at least in our eyes). Zechariah 4:10 (NASB) asks, "For who has despised the day of small things?" Martyn Lloyd-Jones comments that "the small things are, nevertheless, the things of God. Some of God's things are very small, but they are God's; and if you do away with all the small things in the world the big things will soon collapse."[5]

When we get discouraged and begin to imagine that what we're doing isn't worthwhile, we need someone else around to counter the discouragement. When we start listening to ourselves and to the enemy, we're in trouble. If we are alone, it's easy to cycle down into discouragement and depression because we are only a small cog in the wheel.

A what? Actually, a "cog" is a projection on the edge of a gearwheel that engages with corresponding parts on another wheel to transfer motion from one wheel to another. If you don't think that a small cog is important, then watch what happens when it breaks. Everything comes to a screeching halt!

In the battle of life, discouragement is often defeated by the insight of a close friend. One wise, timely word can pull you up out of the swamp— and on you go with a new perspective. And that's why two are better than one.

Now let's get back to the story, laid out for us in Joshua 2:

> And Joshua the son of Nun sent two men secretly from Shittim as spies, saying, "Go, view the land, especially Jericho." And they went and came into the house of a prostitute whose name was Rahab and lodged there. And it was told to the king of Jericho, "Behold, men of Israel have come here tonight to search out the land." Then the king of Jericho sent to Rahab, saying, "Bring out the men who have come to you, who entered your house, for they have come to search out all the land." But the woman had taken the two men and hidden them. And she said, "True,

the men came to me, but I did not know where they were from. And when the gate was about to be closed at dark, the men went out. I do not know where the men went. Pursue them quickly, for you will overtake them." But she had brought them up to the roof and hid them with the stalks of flax that she had laid in order on the roof. So the men pursued after them on the way to the Jordan as far as the fords. And the gate was shut as soon as the pursuers had gone out. (vv. 1–7)

Let's get something straight. I don't want to deal with Rahab and the fact that she lied to protect the spies. Volumes and volumes have been written on that question. Is it an important question? Yes. Am I going to deal with it? No.

I want to deal with the two spies.

So who were these two men?

We don't have a clue about their identities. We don't know their names, we don't know their backgrounds, and we have no idea which of the twelve tribes they belonged to.

All we know about them is their character. It's from their character that we get to know these men and find out what they really were like. Joshua knew these men. He knew their character firsthand. After the fiasco that had happened forty years earlier, do you think he was going to just randomly choose two untested community organizers? Do you think he was going to organize an election and a secret ballot? There was no way he was going to do that. He looked for two men whom he could trust to handle this critical mission. And in looking for two men, he looked first at their character.

We can make at least five observations about the character of the two spies.

- They were willing to risk their lives.
- They had been tested and refined.
- They didn't seek or need the spotlight.
- They were careful about their integrity.
- They were sexually disciplined.

Let's break these down one at a time.

1. They were willing to risk their lives.

The dictionary describes "boldness" as being willing and eager to face danger or adventure with a sense of confidence and fearlessness. I think that's a pretty good description of these two spies. They were willing to walk right through the gates of the Death Star in order to get as much critical information and intelligence as possible.

This is precisely what the apostle Paul would do when he took his missionary journeys around the Roman Empire. He would walk into a city, look for the Jewish synagogue, and begin declaring that Jesus was the Son of God and the Lamb of God. That took a lot of guts, especially since the response wasn't always real positive. Paul said that he had been beaten so many times that he couldn't even put a number on it (2 Cor. 11:23). In other words, he'd stopped counting! That was often the response that he received for declaring that Jesus was the Messiah. That's why Paul specifically asked that the churches would pray for him that he might continue to demonstrate boldness (Phil. 1:19–20).

It takes a bold man and a brave man to keep putting himself in the line of fire. Paul never wanted to get to a point where he was just playing it safe. And that's precisely the attitude that these two spies had as they made their way into Jericho.

Back in the 1950s, a legendary US Air Force fighter pilot named John Boyd had a standing offer to all comers. In a simulated dogfight, he bet that he would be on the other pilot's tail putting him in killing position within forty seconds. If he lost, he would fork out forty dollars. But he never lost. And that's how he got his nickname, "Forty Seconds."

In later years, he became one of the greatest military strategists in history. He's best known for the acronym: OODA, an approach he used and taught to other pilots for air combat. OODA stands for Observe, Orient, Decide, Act. That's the key to becoming a great fighter pilot. It's also the key to leading in any kind of crisis.

Robert Coram writes that "Boyd was famous for a maneuver he called 'flat-plating the bird.' He would be in the defensive position with a challenger tight on his tail, both pulling heavy Gs, when he would suddenly pull the stick full aft, brace his elbows on either side of the cockpit, so the stick would not move laterally, and stomp the rudder. It was as if a manhole cover was sailing through the air and then suddenly flipped 90 degrees. The underside of the fuselage, wings, and horizontal stabilizer became a speed brake that slowed the Hun from 400 knots to 150 knots in seconds. The pursuing pilot was thrown forward and now Boyd was on his tail radioing 'Guns. Guns. Guns.'

"Boyd was equally famous in the classroom where he developed the 'Aerial Attack Study.' Until Boyd came along, fighter pilots thought that air combat was an art rather than a science; that it could never be codified. Boyd proved them wrong when he demonstrated that for every maneuver there is a series of counter maneuvers. And furthermore, there is a counter to every counter. Afterward, when fighter pilots attacked (or were attacked), they knew every option open to their adversary and how to respond."[6]

Charlie Martin takes Boyd's theory and breaks it down into two parts. One of them is the "envelope"—the parameters within which a fighter airplane must operate. The envelope can be seen as a sort of egg-shape, based on how quickly a plane can turn and maneuver. If your plane has a "tighter envelope" than another plane, the pilot has the advantage in a dogfight: You can turn inside the other plane, which means you can get into the perfect firing position, behind the opponent.

More important is the "OODA loop"—which is the envelope for the pilot's thought process. How quickly can the pilot observe the situation, orient within the situation, decide, and act? If the pilot's OODA loop time is shorter, the pilot can overcome the slower.[7]

It takes boldness and bravery to pull this OODA stuff off. When Joshua sent the two spies into Jericho, these guys got into the minds of the enemy and just flat out out-thought them. It was a classic case of observe, orient, decide, and act.

2. They had been tested and refined.

Can I prove to you that they had been tested and refined? No, I can't. I'm not able to take you to a particular passage of Scripture that gives us the details of how each of these men had been prepared for such a task. But do you really think General Joshua would have entrusted such a critical mission to a couple guys who had never been tested?

Joshua was a wiser man than that.

If anybody understood how important it was to send tested, reliable men on a critical recon mission, it was he.

I don't believe Joshua played a lot of tic-tac-toe or solitaire during those forty years in the wilderness. Faithful soldier and servant of Moses that he was, I'm sure he was alert to everything God wanted to teach him. And you can bet that he always had his eye out for young men in the upcoming generation whom he could rely on—men who had been through the fire and passed the test. He was looking for bold and brave young men who had a strong trust in the living God.

When the two spies went into Jericho, they were going in to save a specific woman and her family. Now they didn't know this when Joshua sent them. Joshua didn't brief them on this woman because Joshua didn't know about her. But when they met Rahab the prostitute and agreed to make a covenant with her, you get a glimpse into the fact that these two men had been refined and tested. In Joshua 2:14 the men, after reaching an agreement with Rahab, make this statement:

> And the men said to her, "Our life for yours even to death! If you do not tell this business of ours, *then when the LORD gives us the land* we will deal kindly and faithfully with you."

That phrase "then when the LORD gives us the land" is the tip that they had been tested and refined. These guys had seen the faithfulness of God in the wilderness. They knew of God's great power in the sending of the ten plagues upon Egypt and opening the Red Sea for their people to pass through. They knew that God was a God who could be trusted. Notice that they didn't say *if* God gives us the land. No, it was *when* He gives us the land. As far as they were concerned, it was already an accomplished fact. There was a certainty of faith that only comes from the process of testing and refining. These men were fit for the task.

I recently read a statement from a very well-known Christian singer and songwriter. After thirty-some years of marriage and four children, he was declaring himself to be a homosexual. This guy was very influential in the Christian world—he has sold millions of CDs. He explained that he had been dealing with homosexual desires since he was a kid. Through the years he continued to battle temptation even as he enjoyed a strong marriage. But in the article, he stated that he just got tired of the battle. The sexual temptation was strong and took almost all of his emotional energy on a daily basis. He fought off depression and began to take anti-depressants. As the years turned into decades, he got weary of fighting off temptation. It just wouldn't go away—the battle raged every day. So he decided that the best thing for him to do was to simply "come out" and acknowledge that he is gay. The statement says he's now planning to start "dating" other men.

I want to handle this carefully and discreetly. I'm praying that this guy will return to the Lord, so I'm not going to disclose his name. A friend of mine recently commented on this man's decision in his blog. I'm going to keep his name and his blog under wraps as well, even as I reference one of his observations. Again, the reason I'm doing this is in hopes that some godly men can get to this guy and save him from this wrong decision (Gal. 6:1; James 5:19–20).

The blog writer laid out a very interesting scenario that went something like this. Imagine that there was a gifted Christian teacher who had been dealing with sexual lust toward women since he was a young boy. Even as a young man he had gotten heavily involved in pornography. Every time he saw a beautiful woman, he would immediately fantasize about what she would look like naked and what it would be like to have sex with her. This gifted preacher married a godly woman and together they had four wonderful children. He loved his wife, even though he daily battled the lust for other women. At times he battled so hard that he went into depression. He actually began to take antidepressants. And then one day he announced that he was leaving his wife because he was an adulterer.

Now the interesting thing about this scenario is that the man had never committed adultery. But he was so tired of fighting off lust that he decided deep in his heart he had always been a heterosexual adulterer. So now he was going to go ahead and simply pursue the lifestyle.

Do you see the point?

Just because you are continually tempted doesn't mean that's what you are in your core. We are all sinful in our hearts, and susceptible to different kinds of temptations. Some guys are tempted by homosexuality; the majority of guys are tempted by lust for women. But just because you've grown weary in the battle is no reason to give in to sin. That doesn't make any sense at all. That's nothing more than a way to rationalize sinful behavior.

Suffering and hardship are tools in the hands of God to refine us. Sure you'll struggle, and so will I. We'll struggle until the Lord finally takes us home to heaven, where we'll finally be freed from the battle with sin. But in the meantime, we'll keep on fighting ... day by day, hour by hour, sometimes minute by minute. We'll fight by being in the Word every day and submitting our hearts and our temptations to the Lord. That's the Christian life. But the struggle is never an excuse to give up and go into sin and unbelief.

The two spies knew that the Lord would give Israel the ultimate victory. They didn't know how long it would take, or even if they would be alive to see the final victory. But they knew that God would be faithful and fulfill His promise. And in the meantime, they were going to continue fighting the good fight. Giving up or giving in simply wasn't an option.

3. They didn't seek or need the spotlight.

One of the things that strikes me about these two spies is that they took on a dangerous mission, completed it, gave a positive report to Joshua, and then seemingly disappeared. Joshua 2 is the account of all that they risked and successfully accomplished, and the only other mention of them is in Joshua 6 when the walls came down and they went in to take the city. Joshua 6:22–23 (NASB) gives the play by play:

Joshua said to the two men who had spied out the land,
"Go into the harlot's house and bring the woman and
all she has out of there, as you have sworn to her." So
the young men who were spies went in and brought out
Rahab and her father and her mother and her brothers
and all she had; they also brought out all her relatives and
placed them outside the camp of Israel.

Never again do we hear of these two young men.[8] They did their
job and simply faded into the background. They didn't get an Emmy, an
Oscar, a Grammy, a Tony, or a Golden Globe. They didn't get a star on the
Hollywood Walk of Fame.

The Lord Jesus Christ Himself only ministered in the public eye for
approximately three years. What was He doing before He took on His
public ministry? He was working as an unknown carpenter. Chuck Colson
makes a startling point:

Jesus spent most of His life engaged in manual labor. The
Christian apologist Justin Martyr said that during his
lifetime, back in Galilee in the second century it was still
common to see farmers using plows made by the carpenter Jesus of Nazareth.

In his book *The Call*, theologian Os Guinness reminds
us that even the humblest work is important if done for
God. "How intriguing," Guinness writes, "to think of
Jesus' plow rather than His Cross—to wonder what it
was that made His plows and yokes last and stand out."
Clearly, they must have been made well if they were still
in use in the second century.

Today, Christians typically exalt spiritual work above

manual work. After all, what is making a plow compared
with preaching to multitudes, feeding the five thousand,
or raising someone from the dead? But the very fact that
Jesus did make plows—and made them well—suggests
that any work can be done to the glory of God.[9]

Before Jesus did His first miracle, turning the water into the wine at the
wedding at Cana, He simply worked with wood. He wasn't in the spotlight
and He wasn't speaking to crowds. He was making plows. And He didn't
take shortcuts with the plows. He made them to the best of His ability. He
put such time and quality into His work that they were still being used a
hundred years after His resurrection. He died for the glory of God and He
made plows to the glory of God.

So what kind of work do you do? Are you obscure? Are you unknown?
Then thank God for the blessing of a quiet life (1 Thess. 4:11–12) and get
on with serving Him. He knows who you are, He knows where you are,
and you are working for Him.

4. They were careful about their integrity.

When they showed up at Rahab's house, it became obvious very quickly
that here was a woman who was trusting in the God of Israel. Hebrews
11:30–31 makes it very clear that she was expressing her faith in God when
she hid the men in order to save their lives. Before she hid the men on the
roof, she declared her trust in the One True God:

Before the men lay down, she came up to them on the
roof and said to the men, "I know that the LORD has given
you the land, and that the fear of you has fallen upon us,

and that all the inhabitants of the land melt away before
you. For we have heard how the LORD dried up the water
of the Red Sea before you when you came out of Egypt,
and what you did to the two kings of the Amorites who
were beyond the Jordan, to Sihon and Og, whom you
devoted to destruction. And as soon as we heard it, our
hearts melted, and there was no spirit left in any man
because of you, for the LORD your God, he is God in the
heavens above and on the earth beneath. Now then, please
swear to me by the LORD that, as I have dealt kindly with
you, you also will deal kindly with my father's house, and
give me a sure sign that you will save alive my father and
mother, my brothers and sisters, and all who belong to
them, and deliver our lives from death." (Josh. 2:8–13)

Now watch how carefully the two spies respond to her. They are very
clear in laying out the terms of their agreement with her.

And the men said to her, "Our life for yours even to death!
If you do not tell this business of ours, then when the
LORD gives us the land we will deal kindly and faithfully
with you."

Then she let them down by a rope through the window, for her house was built into the city wall, so that she
lived in the wall. And she said to them, "Go into the hills,
or the pursuers will encounter you, and hide there three
days until the pursuers have returned. Then afterward you
may go your way." The men said to her, "We will be guiltless with respect to this oath of yours that you have made
us swear. Behold, when we come into the land, you shall

tie this scarlet cord in the window through which you let
us down, and you shall gather into your house your father
and mother, your brothers, and all your father's house-
hold. Then if anyone goes out of the doors of your house
into the street, his blood shall be on his own head, and we
shall be guiltless. But if a hand is laid on anyone who is
with you in the house, his blood shall be on our head. But
if you tell this business of ours, then we shall be guiltless
with respect to your oath that you have made us swear."
And she said, "According to your words, so be it." Then
she sent them away, and they departed. And she tied the
scarlet cord in the window. (vv. 14–21)

This was the covenant they made with Rahab. And to their credit, they
were as good as their word. They clarified their agreement and repeated
what they would do and what circumstances would release them from the
covenant. That's integrity.

Several years ago, a well-known Christian songwriter announced that
he had been diagnosed with a very aggressive strain of cancer. Letters of
sympathy and commitments to prayer came in from all over the world.
A Web site was set up and donations were accepted to help him with his
medical costs. He then wrote a song proclaiming the fact that God was
our Healer, and it became a smash hit. He would sing it to packed out
auditoriums of believers whose hearts ached as he performed with oxygen
tubes in his nose and a cane in his hand to keep him steady.

He told how his wife would get up in the middle of night to microwave
hot towels to put on his back and relieve his suffering.

He admitted two weeks ago that the whole thing was a fraud.

He never had cancer. Never. It was all a big con, and it has shaken many
Christians to the core. A shaken family member announced that the man was

getting treatment for his sickness. It's not sickness—it's dishonesty. It is sin. It was all premeditated, planned, and carefully choreographed. Oxygen tubes and a cane—that's not an illness—that's pure deception. But the crowds were moved beyond words when he stood in the spotlight leaning on that cane.

Joshua had seen the effects and consequences of ten men who were in sin. He had seen how it had impacted the entire nation. So he made sure when he chose the two that he knew their hearts and their track record. He couldn't afford to give dishonest men such responsibility. The stakes were simply too high.

5. They were sexually disciplined.

When the spies got to Jericho, they spent the night at the home of a woman by the name of Rahab. She lived in one of the houses that had been erected right by the outside wall, so her house was a good place to work from. It was also a brothel, and it was not uncommon for men—unknown men— to be coming and going. It was the perfect cover. Now there was just one problem. Rahab was a prostitute. And it was in the house of a prostitute that these two men stayed overnight. Now I have a question for you: What if these two men had approached Rahab to have sex with them? That would have been an incredibly wicked thing to do.

Now let's be clear here—they didn't proposition Rahab. But knowing her profession, they certainly could have. So why didn't they? The answer is that they were circumcised in their hearts. They were men who were obedient to the Lord from the heart. They weren't yet circumcised in their flesh, because that happened after the crossing of the Jordan. They spent the night at Rahab's before the crossing, therefore they had not taken the mark on their sexual organs. But they had taken the mark on their hearts. They wanted to live lives of holiness before the Lord.

Because they had taken the mark in their hearts, it came out in their behavior. And they did nothing in Rahab's home that was not honorable.

Rahab was a woman who heard of the great God who opened the Red Sea for the children of Israel—and she wanted to know Him. This woman and her family were saved when Jericho was destroyed. She trusted in the Lord and became the great-great-grandmother of David, Israel's greatest king (Matt. 1:5–6).

What if these two men were not living in holiness? What if they had not been circumcised in their hearts? You can easily imagine they might have made indecent advances to Rahab. After all, they knew her profession. They easily could have turned her from the Lord by their wicked intentions. But they didn't; these were men of holiness and obedience. Joshua trusted them, and they proved themselves worthy of his trust.

This woman Rahab, along with her family, became part of Israel. She married a man named Salmon. They had a son. His name was Boaz and he married a woman named Ruth. Her story is told in the Old Testament book that bears her name. Boaz and Ruth had a son named Obed. Obed in turn had a son he named Jesse. And then Jesse had six sons—and the youngest he named David.

Rahab the prostitute was the great-great-grandmother of David, the great king of Israel. Do you see why the character of the two spies was so important when they encountered this prostitute who wanted to know the Lord?

I have a friend who was molested by a worship leader when he was ten years old. It happened at a church youth camp, and the incident threw him into sexual confusion for years. When he graduated from high school, he went to a Christian college, where he found himself continuing to struggle with homosexual temptation. He knew that kind of behavior was wrong, but couldn't understand why he was so drawn to it. He desperately wanted to be used by the Lord, and wanted to do the right thing. But he was terribly conflicted. He wanted wisdom and godly counsel, so he went to the college chaplain and told him his struggle with temptation. The chaplain listened very carefully—and then propositioned him for sex right there in the chapel.

Here's a nineteen-year-old kid trying to fight off sin. He looks for a trusted counselor to help him get closer to the Lord. And he is invited by that trusted counselor to engage in the very act he was trying to flee from.

Thank God that he was rescued from this demonic predator. And thank God that the two spies were men that Rahab could trust to lead her to the God of Israel.

I don't know the names of these two men.

But I sure want to live like they lived.

Chapter Twelve

God Is My Banker

"Grace makes the promise and providence the payment."
—*John Flavel*

I started working on this book over a year ago.

And in that time the wealth of the world has been nearly cut in half.[1]

At the time of this writing, the economic meltdown doesn't appear to be going away anytime in the near future. So I would suggest that we pay very close attention to two statements that Joshua made toward the end of his life. These two statements are the keys to navigating economic uncertainty.

The first are the well-known words that he uttered in Joshua 24:15: *"As for me and my house, we will serve the LORD."*

In other words, Joshua had given the Lord first place in his life. Joshua isn't serving the Lord as an afterthought—the Lord is first in his heart and mind. The Lord is the Master and Joshua is His obedient servant.

The second principle that Joshua uttered is actually found in two different verses—owing to the fact that Joshua stated the same principle on two different occasions.

Facing the obstacles and giants in their path, Joshua and Caleb not only had a conviction that God would fulfill His promise, they *acted* on that conviction. Their character was based on God's character—they knew He wouldn't lie to them. They knew that He would keep His promises.

This is confirmed years later as Joshua speaks his last words to the nation. Last words are important. And as Joshua approached the end of his life, he had one final thought that he wanted to imprint on the minds of those who would read his account.

So he laid it out on the table—twice. Just so we couldn't miss it.

The first is in Joshua 21:45:

"Not one word of all the good promises that the LORD had made to the house of Israel had failed; all came to pass."

The second is found in Joshua 23:14:

"And now I am about to go the way of all the earth, and you know in your hearts and souls, all of you, that not one word has failed of all the good things that the LORD your God promised concerning you. All have come to pass for you; not one of them has failed."

Joshua lived to be 110 years old. And in that 110 years he never saw God fail to fulfill His promise—never. Joshua and Caleb believed God's promise to help them drive out the giants—and He did.

We started this book with the acknowledgment that we are living in days of tremendous financial uncertainty. We are watching an economic meltdown take place before our eyes. Everything that seemed secure is now in question.

So how in the world do we face the future with any kind of sanity and hope? I would suggest that we do exactly the same thing that Joshua prescribed: We put the Lord first in our lives, and we live off of His promises on a daily basis.

That, in essence, is the message of Matthew 6:33. It is in that verse where the Lord Jesus summarizes His teaching on how to defeat anxiety and worry about the future. To be more specific, He speaks directly to how one would survive *economically* in the days ahead. He deals head-on with toxic worry about how we are going to provide food, clothing, and shelter for our families. And you can also throw in worries about paying your mortgage and putting your kids through college. It's all covered under the umbrella statement in Matthew 6:25 that the Lord Jesus used to introduce His teaching on anxiety: *Don't worry about your life.*

So what do we do? We worry about our lives. We worry about losing our jobs, saving for retirement, and the implications of the United States becoming a socialist state. And to all of these worries and many more, the Lord Jesus says, *Don't do it! Don't let yourself be eaten alive by worries about day-to-day living.* And then in the following verses, He gives us the reasons why we shouldn't worry—based upon the fact that we have a loving Father who intimately knows our every need. I would suggest that you open your Bible often to Matthew 6:25–34, and sear those verses into your mind.

But for our purposes in this closing chapter, I want to home in on the summary principle that the Lord Jesus taught in Matthew 6:33:

> But seek first the kingdom of God and his righteousness,
> and all these things will be added to you.

What I find interesting about this verse is that the Lord Jesus is teaching the exact same two principles that Joshua emphasized. He is telling us to seek the Lord first. That's exactly the same thrust of Joshua's statement— *"As for me and my house, we will serve the LORD."* He serves the Lord because the Lord is *first* in his life.

And then the Lord Jesus makes a promise to all who seek Him first: "And all of these things will be added to you." What things? The things that you need to make it through life—food, clothing, shelter, and all of the other things we worry over.

Joshua said twice that the Lord has never failed to fulfill a promise, and here the Lord is teaching the same thing. As He makes the promise, He guarantees the promise. This is why down through the years so many of God's people have lived off of the promise of Matthew 6:33. I suggest that in these days of economic crisis we follow their example.

The Promises in the Outback

Born in 1903 in Australia, Stacey Woods made his way to Wheaton College in Illinois in 1925. After finishing his education, the Lord used him for the next fifty years in reaching university students all over the United States and Europe with the gospel of Jesus Christ. For all of his adult life he was involved in winning college students to the Lord and grounding them in the Scriptures. In 1975 he wrote his autobiography, *Some Ways of God,* and it is a fascinating read. In his book, he tells how he survived through the years by taking the promise of Matthew 6:33 literally. And he learned to do so from his father:

> My father was converted in Queensland, Australia. In his late teens, after completing a course in architecture, he was called by God to be an itinerant evangelist and Bible teacher....
>
> He would go to a town, often where there was no church, set up his meeting-tent and visit the people house by house, inviting them to the services. Later, when he married, my mother traveled with him, playing a little folding organ and singing. People were converted. He would teach them, rooting them in the Scriptures. A local church would be established with elders and deacons. Father would plan a simple building, and he and the men

of the church would build it. Only then did Father feel free to move on....

Father had a profound trust in God and His promises. He took Matthew 6:33 literally: God had promised to meet his need. He never had a salary, never took up an offering for his ministry nor authorized anyone else to do so, never asked for personal financial support.

This quiet confidence on the part of both of my parents—for Mother stood one hundred percent with Father—made a deep impression on me. Trusting God for everything was part of our life. My parents did not preach one thing and live another. The reverse was almost true. They lived this of faith in God but did not talk about it.[2]

So when God called him to ministry as a young man, Stacey did not ask how God was going to provide for him. He had seen the living God answer prayer all of his life. He had seen Matthew 6:33 lived out before him. Because of the influence of his parents, he learned to put God first and to live off of His promises.

The Promises in the Middle East

When Franklin Graham was a young man and very skeptical about his father's Christianity, he spent some time working as a helper and handyman at very small hospital in the desert of Jordan. This little hospital was the work of two missionary women and a retired farmer from the United States named Lester. These fine people lived daily off of the promises of God. Franklin tells of the impact that they had upon him as he was running from the Lord:

I began to pay close attention to how Aileen and Eleanor took care of the financial needs of the hospital. To be honest, it freaked me out! The ladies never wrote newsletters or sent out appeals. "God knows our needs," Eleanor said more than once. "If God knows, that's all that counts, isn't it?" Who could argue with that?

Every Friday afternoon, which was the Muslim holy day, the two women asked all of us to meet inside the hospital for prayer. The meetings were unforgettable. Someone would read from the Bible and elaborate on what the passage meant. After this study of God's word, a list of prayer requests was made. That's when the missionaries simply asked God to provide whatever was needed.

Sometimes the need was as basic as food. At other times it involved large sums of money for a phase of the construction or for hospital equipment.

Eleanor, Aileen, and Lester would all drop to their knees for a time of earnest prayer. Not once did I see them violate this approach of asking God, in faith, to provide. It must not have been easy for them, yet they never seemed to be in turmoil or to wring their hands in despair. I could not fathom how they lived in such peace in the midst of great need....

One Friday, Eleanor asked that we pray for the Lord to provide funds to pay a medicine bill from a Swedish company. I recall the gist of her plea:

"Lord, You know that we don't have $1,355, but this is Your hospital. Your name is on the line, not ours. If this bill doesn't get paid, it's Your name that gets discredited.

If it pleases You, Lord, and if it be Your will, provide for this need. Amen."

I tried hard not to be cynical, but I couldn't believe that the money would come if no one on the "outside" knew about the need. I thought, if they would just let their needs be known, maybe someone would care enough to help. I had grown to love these women, and I didn't want to see them hurt. But I had completely missed the point; they had already told Someone.

The next Monday an envelope arrived containing a handwritten note, which read: "I have heard about the wonderful work you are doing there, and you have been in my thoughts. I had some extra money and wanted to send it to you. Enclosed is a check. Use it any way you see fit."

The check was for $1,355.

When Eleanor showed it to me, I don't know what was more obvious—my gulp or my eyes bulging out my head. My cynical, immature view of how life worked was taking some major hits. I could not deny the reality of what I was seeing. This kind of thing happened week after week.[3]

George Müller and the Promises

I have referred several times to the work of George Müller in England among the orphans of Bristol. Müller was very careful not to ever make a financial need known to anyone other than the Lord. For over sixty years, this was his way of funding the thousands of orphans under his care. And day by day, week by week, God continued to answer his prayers for financial provision.

But George Müller didn't discover this approach on his own. Over a hundred years prior to Müller's establishing his orphanage in England, there was a man in Germany by the name of August H. Francke. Müller began his orphanage in 1834, but in 1833 he had been given the biography of Francke. In the late 1600s Francke had established an orphanage in Germany that had continued for over a hundred years without Francke's ever making an appeal for financial help to anyone other than the Lord. While many people know of the ministry of George Müller, very few have ever heard of the work of August Francke. Yet it was Francke's model and ministry that motivated Müller to trust God for the finances of his orphanage in England.

Müller could actually picture what such an orphanage that would care for over two thousand orphans would look like, for as a young man he had boarded in Francke's orphanage in Germany for several weeks when he was pursuing biblical training.[4] If Francke could live off of the promises of the living God, then so could George Müller.

Müller was fond of saying over the years that God was his banker, basing that declaration on the promise of Matthew 6:33. "Muller decided that 'Seek first the kingdom of God and His righteousness, and all these things will be added to you': meant something like 'Seek first the kingdom of God and His righteousness, and all these things will be added to you.'"[5] In other words, he took the promise of the Lord Jesus *literally*.

In these days of great uncertainty, our great God wants His people to know that He can be trusted. And He is giving us the opportunity to find out for ourselves that His promises can be trusted. That's what Müller found out firsthand, and it's the reason he wrote his autobiography:

"I have mentioned the answers to prayer that through them (the brethren) may be encouraged to make known their requests unto God ... that they may be stirred up to 'seek first the kingdom of God and His righteousness,' resting assured that, in so doing so, He will give them what is needful for the life that now is."[6]

Today, we live in a world where there is much worry and concern over the status of the banks, the future of social security, and the need for adequate health care. It can be somewhat overwhelming as one attempts to financially plan and provide for the future. In the midst of this unsettling frenzy there is something we all need to know.

God is your banker.

God is your social security.

God is your health-care provider.

You don't need a bigger government.

You have a great God.

And unlike silver-tongued politicians, He can be trusted to keep His promises.

I vote for Him.

Study Questions for Personal Reflection or Small-Group Discussion

Chapter 1: Hard Times

1. What is the question the psalmist asks in Psalm 42:5? How would you answer that question today? What are the big issues in your life today that cause you concern or despair?

   why are you in Dispair, and why have you become Distrubed with in me?
   The Author Says uNcerTaNiTy Family remain strong in there walk uNcerTaNiTy EcoNomy + NaTion

2. In what ways have Americans been living as though the riches of this world are certain? How have you been living that way? What new realities are now challenging that certainty?

   they live as if the sTock market was their God, use the credit card like it was free movey the world + ecomoNy

3. Read Psalm 42:5 again. What is the hope offered in this verse? What are the three certainties that form the (true) foundation of our hope?

   PuT your hope in God my Savior and my God

4. Define "the providence of God." What does God promise us? What doesn't He promise? Read Psalm 103:19 and Proverbs 16:4. How do each of these verses speak to God's providence?

> The Lord has established His throne in Heaven
>
> His Kingdom Rules over all
>
> The Lord works out everything To its proper end.

5. What is the key message of Matthew 6:25? Why do we tend to worry about our lives so much? How does the certainty of God's promises answer our concern and worry? (See Matt. 6:25–34.) Why is it so difficult to trust God's promises?

> DO NOT worry
>
> work, where we live, what we wear, what we drive, our kids, our GraND Kids,
>
> Seek First His Kingdom and His righteousness and all these things will be given To you

6. Why are so many Christians troubled by the prophecies in Revelation? How does our fear of what's to come impact the manner in which we live? What did God tell Jeremiah to do in the face of rapidly approaching hard times? How can we apply that message to our lives today?

> the have NoT accepted God as their FaTher

Chapter 2: Giants

1. What does it mean to "fight the giants"? What sort of giants did the Israelites run into in their journey to the Promised Land? How did God use Joshua and Caleb to "fight the giants"?

   Any Thing That Threatens our peace, well-being and very existence Fear of The giant people Keep Israel from the land God promised Them Joshua and Caleb like David Knew That God Almighty controlled The Giants.

2. Why were the men selected as two of the twelve to go into the land notable? In what way were they "not able"? In what ways were they "panicked leaders"? What are the results of panicked leadership? What examples of this can you note from your own experience?

   They were Not Able To convince the people To Take The land God promised Them. when they could have Keep there eyes on the greatest Giant of all God they wilted before There giants

3. Respond to the following statement: "Every man who desires to be used by God will face the giants." How does that make you feel? What are some examples of biblical characters who faced giants because God was using them? Have you experienced this in your own life? Describe that experience.

   they will either be giants that defeat us or stepping stone To be defeated like David Job, Ester, Jeremiah, Daniel, Jonah Paul, Peter

4. What are the two normal, instinctive responses to a threatening giant?
   How is this observed in the story of the spies? (See Num. 13:31.) Why
   do we so easily focus on our inadequacies? What is the biblical answer
   to these normal responses?

   we can't attack, they are stronger
   then we are.
   Daniel knew the Answer Daniel 2: 20-21

5. What are some of the giants Christians face today? Who is the greatest
   Giant? How does knowing this help you as you face the other giants in
   your life?

   all the things Steve listed
   God is the greatest of all giants

6. What are the three questions the author poses and answers at the end of
   this chapter? Why are they important questions? What do the answers
   say about how we're to approach the giants? How does what we think
   or believe about God impact our battle readiness?

   How much wisdom Does God have
   God has all wisdom

   How much Power Does God have
   God has all Power

Chapter 3: Gravitas

1. Summarize the example from the introduction to this chapter that illustrates the importance of character. Why is it true that "character is never a minor issue"? Describe why character was the primary difference between Joshua and Caleb and the other ten spies.

   we can oo all Things through christ who gives me strenght.
   Joshua and Caleb believed that God was in charge The other Ten Doubted The power they posessed Through God.

2. Review Titus 2:2. In what ways might this be a glimpse into the character of Joshua and Caleb? What is the character "recipe"? What are the four "s" traits the author describes? How have you observed these in leaders you've known? How do you exhibit these traits in your own life at home? At work? Among friends? Strangers?

   Temperate, digntfied, sensible, sound in Faith, in love, in perseverance.
   Sober - Serious - sensible -
   Sound - in Faith, Love, and perseverance

3. What does it mean that God is "self-existent"? Why is that important? (See Ps. 50:10–12.) Read Malachi 3:6. What does this verse teach us about God? What can we conclude about God from this?

   God has always been and will Always Be.
   Everyone Depends on God but God Depends on No one
   God is the Source of Life and the Sustainer of life.
   malachi 3:6 "For I The Lord Do Not change"

4. How does God's "infinite" nature impact the way we view Him? How does this truth help us when dealing with challenges or facing giants? Consider God's "all-knowing-ness." (See Prov. 15:3.) How does God's knowledge help us face challenges?

> God has NO Limits
> we will Display strenght and Take Action
> God Knows all things that are and could be

5. What does it look like to trust God? How does our trust of God put us in a place where God can use us? Think of examples in your own experience where you had a hard time trusting God. Did you sense Him using you during those times? How might your trust of Him have changed the circumstance or results?

> Trusting God is getting To Know God, you cant completly Trust someone with out completly Knowing Them

6. What was your reaction to Paul Lanier's story? How is his story an example of facing giants? Where did Paul get his strength when his body was becoming weak? In what ways did he exemplify a man with gravitas?

> Paul's giant the biggest we face Death.
> His trust + Faith in His savior God.
> He never stopped working for His God and Savior

Chapter 4: Slaves

1. Why is it significant that Joshua and Caleb were born slaves? How did their experience in suffering help prepare them for the roles they would play in the Israelites' story?

2. What are the four giants a man who is a slave must fight? How did David Livingstone fight these giants? How did Joshua and Caleb fight them? In what ways are you a "slave" too? When and where have you encountered these four giants in your own life? *Page 80*

3. Respond to the following statement: "If Christ is your Lord and Savior, then you are not a slave. Nor are you an owner." What does it really mean to be a steward? How does this truth help to mitigate the fears that come when the economy is struggling?

4. What are three things we know about Joshua the slave? Read Romans 5:3. What does this verse teach us about how God prepares His leaders for difficult circumstances?

5. Why are we to rejoice in our sufferings? How do we do that? Is it easy? Why or why not? How does Romans 5:1–5 help us see why we can rejoice in our sufferings?

6. Read Ephesians 2:10. How does knowing that God has a plan for you help you when you face seasons of life when you see little or no results? Have you lost your dreams in these times? What caused that lack of faith? How does God use seasons of barrenness to prepare men?

Chapter 5: Increased Hardship

1. What is the author's observation about nearly every person whose biography he has read? Why do you think this is true? What are the two possible responses a man can have when facing increased hardship?

   They have Faced Hardships That either makes them or breaks them.
   IT can be The Fire that perofies
   The hardship can make or break
   The person

2. What was the "straw that broke the camel's back" in the Israelites' story? (See Ex. 5.) What giants were they fighting while in captivity? Why might the Israelites have blamed God for their circumstances?

   The people had To supply their own
   straw To make the bricks Demanded
   by Pharaoh. Their work was almost Doubled
   but The production Needed To be The Same
   INdirectly they were asking the Lord To
   Judge mose for making them Stink before Pharaoh

3. What are the possible responses to increased hardship that seemingly comes from God? What is the "brokenness" that comes from difficult circumstances? How can brokenness lead to fruitfulness? How did this happen in the lives of the Israelites? How have you experienced this in your own life?

   Hard ship can lead To bitterness
   or brokenness
   this brokeness can lead To fruitfulness
   Brokeness is the process by which
   God dislodges our Self. life and Teaches
   us To rely upon Him alone in every
   Facet of our lives.

4. Read 2 Corinthians 1:8–10. What are some ways you can relate to the message of this passage? How have you been "burdened beyond your strength"? How has the giant of increased hardship appeared in your life?

> we depend on our own skills and abilities when things are goin good we Turn To God when the Task is To great For us to Handle

5. What observations did Frank W. Boreham make in a sermon on Benaiah? How did Benaiah respond to his horribly difficult circumstances? What allowed him to "take care of business" even though the odds were stacked against him?

> He met the worst of enemies
> In the worst of Places
> In the worst conditions
> God showed Benaiah Victory in
> The worst of Times As He promises
> To Do For us only Trust

6. Respond to the following statement: "Facing the giant of increased hardship means that deliverance is right around the corner—maybe." Read 2 Corinthians 1:9–10. What does Paul report about his deliverance? Why do some people turn bitter when facing increased hardship? How does bitterness affect our ability to do God's work?

> His hardship came so He would Trust in our father God and Not on His strength for Victory
> God Delivered and will Deliver again + again
> Not Always on our Time but always on God's Time
> Patient in The Lord

Chapter 6: Circling the Airport

1. How do you think Joshua and Caleb felt after being spared the plague that killed the other ten spies? Why do you think God still chose to let the Israelites wander in the wilderness another forty years?

2. What are some examples in your own life where God didn't seem to make sense to you? Read Isaiah 55:8. How does this verse speak to our understanding of God's ways?

3. What are the three things every man who encounters the giant of maintenance and monotony must become acquainted with? What does it mean that God works "in" you before He works "through" you?

4. What are some of the life disappointments you've experienced? How might God have used those disappointments to shape your life? In what way have you known the truth espoused in Proverbs 13:12: "Hope deferred makes the heart sick, but desire fulfilled is the tree of life"? Why does deferred hope make us heartsick? What role does trusting God play in these seasons of life?

5. How does the story of the dog training relate to your own experience with what it means to "stay"? Do you prefer to be "where the action is"? Why or why not? Why is the command "stay" so hard to obey?

6. What are the six phases of leadership development Dr. J. Robert Clinton describes in his book *The Making of a Leader*? What transitions have you experienced (or are you anticipating) as you mature in your faith life? Who is responsible for the transitions? How will you know when it's time for a transition? What are some practical things you can do to recognize and be ready for those transitions?

Chapter 7: High Wire Promotion

1. In what ways did the forty years in the wilderness take its toll on the Israelites? How did the transition to Joshua's leadership take place at the end of that forty years? (See Josh. 1:1–9.)

2. What is your reaction to the statement that "every leader is replaceable"? How does God apply this truth to the story of the Israelites? What does this say about God's sovereign plan? God's timing?

3. What is significant about the promotion that Joshua got? How did he get this promotion? (See Num. 27:15–23.) What lessons can we extract from how God worked in this story? (See also Ps. 75.)

4. What is the "good ambition" that Paul references in 2 Corinthians 5:9? What is the root of this ambition? How does this compare to what the author calls "arsenic" ambition? (See James 3:13–17.)

5. Describe the greatest problem with "the high wire of promotion." What is the compass a Christian man must trust in life? How does this compass help us make good choices in the area of promotion and leadership? What are the three coordinates God gave Joshua in 1:1–9?

6. Why is it so important to know God's Word? Read Psalm 119:105. What are some of the promises you know well? How have they helped you to be bold and courageous? To make wise decisions?

Chapter 8: The Worst Possible Time

1. Briefly summarize the stories of Dave Ramsey and Patrick Morley. How did these men respond to the challenges of the Tax Reform Act? What surprised you most about these stories? Where do you see God in these stories?

2. What were the two water crossings that Joshua and Caleb experienced? What is significant about the second crossing? Why does the author state that there are no "unforeseen events"? What are examples of events that may have seemed "unforeseen" in your own life?

3. How do unforeseen (by us) events impact us? What are the challenges they present? What are the possible benefits they can bring? Respond to the following quote: "God sometimes raises difficulties in the lives of His people that He may have the glory of subduing them and helping His people over them."

4. Why did the Israelites find themselves in crisis in the Red Sea event? What was the cause? What clues do we have from Scripture that help us see this was an event planned by God for His purposes? What were the results of this event in the lives of God's people?

5. Read Exodus 14:17–18; Matthew 6:9; Psalm 9:10; and Proverbs 18:10. What do all these verses tell us about honoring God's name? What does that look like in today's culture? How do we honor God's name?

6. Summarize the author's "house selling" story. How do you see God being honored in that story? What are some similar examples of God being honored through seemingly ordinary events in your life or the lives of people you know? What does this tell you about how God works His plan?

Chapter 9: Fighting Off Fear

1. Respond to the following quote: "Manliness, like suffering, deals with fear.... Manly men rise above their fear, but in doing so they carry their fear with them, though it is under control." What does it mean that men "carry their fear with them"?

2. What responsibility did God give Joshua just before they entered the Promised Land? What four commands were going to be required of him? What does Ephesians 6:11 tell us about why it's important to be on constant guard?

3. Why do you think God commanded Joshua to lead the Israelites across the river at the worst possible time? How does doing this demonstrate God's greatness? What are similar experiences you've had that seemed like the "worst possible time" for you to do something? In what ways was God glorified through those experiences?

4. What was the point of God's command to the Israelites to "camp and contemplate"? Why did God command the leaders to go first or to stay in harm's way? How do these commands apply to our lives today? In what current life situation do you hear God calling you to "camp and contemplate"? To "go first" and "stay in harm's way"?

5. What is the point of the "stacked stones"? (See Josh. 4.) What is significant about the process by which the twelve men collected and stacked the stones? What are the "stacked stones" in your life? What legacy do you hope to leave your children?

6. Review the author's story about the ranch that closes this chapter. What stands out to you about this story? Where do you see God in it? How did God use the author's life (and the lives of others) to bring glory to Himself?

Chapter 10: Three Tasks

1. What are the three consistent actions God requires of those who say "Use me!"? In what ways were these important truths for Joshua? How do they apply to you today?

Take the mark
Trust His Provision
Take a knee

2. What is the "giant of complete vulnerability"? How does God "show up" when we're facing this giant? What was this giant for the Israelites? What does this giant look like in your life?

> They were under the mercy of God for their protection
>
> We See how helpless our Nation is Today as our hearts move Further away From the protective Hand of God

3. How does "circumcision in heart" affect a man? Respond to the following statement: "Everything within Christianity is an issue of the heart." Do you agree? (Read Deut. 6:5 and Rom. 10:6–10.)

> We believe and are justified by our heart and we confess our Sin Fulness + are saved by the confession of our mouths To Jesus.

4. Read Psalm 55:22. In what way does this verse speak to the issue of fear? What does it mean to be "sustained" (P 213) by the Lord? Is it easy to trust God's sustenance? Why or why not?

> Cast what He has given you upon The Lord and He will Sustain you.

5. Look at Joshua 5:10–12. What does this passage tell you about God's provision? What are some examples from your own experience where you've been the recipient of God's provision? What is your "daily bread" today?

> the manna ceased on this Day Jesus replaced The manna with food produced From the Land.

6. Describe what the author means by "take a knee." What prompted Joshua to take a knee in Joshua 5:13–15? Moses, in Exodus 3:5? How are these examples of what it means to submit to God? In what ways are you on "holy ground" today? What ought your response be to that truth?

Complete Surrender To christ in your life

Any where christ The Lord is is Holy Ground

geT in Line with our commander and chief

Chapter 11: Two Spies

1. In what ways was Jericho like the Death Star? How would you have responded if God had given you the instructions He gave Joshua in Joshua 6:1–5? How did Joshua respond?

2. The author contends that the conquest of Jericho actually began in the second chapter of Joshua. What is his reasoning? Why does Joshua pick just two men to spy on Jericho instead of twelve, or for that matter, one? (See Eccl. 4:9.)

3. What are some of the reasons "two are stronger than one"? What are the enemy's greatest weapons against a man who desires to be used for God's glory? How have you experienced this? If you've also experienced the strength that comes from "two," describe one or more of those situations.

4. What are the five observations the author makes about Jericho's spies? What other observations/conclusions can you make about these men and their character? Why do you think character was so important when choosing the spies? In what ways were the Jericho spies "tested and refined"? How do you see these traits in your own life? What brings testing and refinement?

5. Respond to the following statement: "Just because you are continually tempted doesn't mean that's what you are in your core." Do you agree? Disagree? Why?

6. Why do so many men seek the spotlight? What does it say about a person's character if he seeks notoriety for his actions? Are you a spotlight seeker? If so, what are some practical things you can do to refocus your attention on giving God the glory instead? (See 1 Thess. 4:11–12.)

Chapter 12: God Is My Banker

1. What was the most significant thing you learned about Joshua and Caleb's faith journey? How can their example of "fighting the giants" help you as you face your own giants? What aspect of their story is most inspiring to you? Most challenging?

2. Respond to the following quote: "Character is formed in relation to convictions and it is manifested in the capacity to abide by those convictions even in, especially in, the face of temptation." How does God fit into this definition of character? What are the "layers" of character God is forming within you?

3. When you started reading this book, how concerned were you about
   the current economic situation? How has the content of this book
   affected your level of concern?

4. Think about the giants you're facing today—economic, relational,
   emotional, or otherwise. How much of the battle are you taking upon
   yourself? In what ways are you trusting God to help you fight the
   battle? Are there some practical steps you can take that will force you
   to trust God more? What are they? Think about taking those steps in
   the coming weeks.

5. Read James 2:15–17. If you are in a season of surplus, how are you
   using that surplus? What would it look like to trust God with those
   resources? How might God be glorified by your actions?

6. The author states that God never failed to come through on a promise to Joshua. Reflect on this in your own life. If there are areas where you're unsure about God's role, step back and consider ways He might be testing you or stretching you or preparing you for battle. How might God glorify Himself through your current trials?

Notes

Chapter 1

1. Ira Stoll, *Samuel Adams: A Life* (New York: Free, 2008), 3.
2. http://online.wsj.com/article/SB122169431617549947.html.
3. Sir John Glubb, cited by Guy R. Odom, *Mothers, Leadership and Success* (Houston: Polybius, 1990), 186.
4. http://dariusthemede.tripod.com/glubb/.
5. Ron Mehl, *God Works the Night Shift* (Colorado Springs, CO: Multnomah, 2006).
6. http://www.reformed.org/documents/index.html?mainframe=http://www.reformed.org/documents/heidelberg.html.
7. Charles Colson and Harold Fickett, *The Faith* (Grand Rapids, MI: Zondervan, 2008), 101.
8. George Müller, *Autobiography of George Müller* (Denton, TX: Westminster Literature Resources, 2003), 382.
9. Ibid.

Chapter 2

1. Jay Wink, *The Great Upheaval* (New York: HarperCollins, 2007), 115. Thomas Jefferson referred to the Assembly of Notables in France as the "not ables."
2. C. F. Keil and F. Delitzsch, *Commentary on the Old Testament in Ten Volumes, Volume 1* (Grand Rapids, MI: William B. Eerdmans, 1980), 89, 91.
3. See 2 Samuel 21:17.
4. See 2 Samuel 21:15–17.
5. See 2 Samuel 21:18.
6. 1 Chronicles 20:5; 2 Samuel 21:19.

7. Frank Zappa, cited in *The International Thesaurus of Quotations*, compiled by Eugene Ehrlich and Marshall DeBruhl (New York: Harper Collins, 1996), 660.

8. J. I. Packer, *Knowing God* (Downers Grove, IL: InterVarsity, 1973), 91.

9. Wayne Grudem, *Systematic Theology* (Grand Rapids, MI: Zondervan, 1994), 216.

10. Ibid., 217.

11. Ephesians 6:10.

12. D. Martyn Lloyd-Jones, *The Christian Soldier: An Exposition of Ephesians 6:10–20* (Grand Rapids, MI: Baker, 1977), 17.

13. Job 23:14 NASB.

14. John J. Murray, *Behind a Frowning Providence* (Carlisle, PA: The Banner of Truth Trust, 1990), 10.

Chapter 3

1. Dinesh D'Souza, *What's So Great About Christianity* (Washington, DC: Regnery, 2007), 141.

2. http://www.atomicarchive.com/Bios/Oppenheimer.shtml.

3. Malcolm Gladwell, *Outliers: The Story of Success* (New York: Little, Brown and Company, 2008), 98.

4. Ibid.

5. All Churchill citations from James C. Humes, *The Wit and Wisdom of Winston Churchill* (New York: HarperCollins, 1994), 148–55.

6. Cleon L. Rogers, Jr. and Cleon L. Rogers III, *The New Linguistic and Exegetical Key to the Greek New Testament* (Grand Rapids, MI: Zondervan, 1998), 509.

7. Gene Getz, *The Measure of a Man* (Glendale, CA: Gospel Light, 1974), 38.

8. Ibid., 46.

9. J. D. Douglas and Philip Comfort, ed., *Who's Who in Christian History* (Wheaton, IL: Tyndale, 1992), 735.

10. John D. Woodbridge, ed., *Great Leaders of the Christian Church* (Chicago: Moody, 1988), 177.

11. Louis Berkhof, *A Summary of Christian Doctrine* (Carlisle, PA: The Banner of Truth Trust, 2002), 30.

12. Num. 23:19; Ps. 33:11; 102:27; Mal. 3:6; Heb. 6:17; James 1:17. Berkhof, *A Summary of Christian Doctrine*, 30.

13. Berkhof, *A Summary of Christian Doctrine*, 31.

14. 1 Kings 8:27; Ps. 139:7–10; Isa. 66:1; Jer. 23:23; Acts 17:27–28. Berkhof, *A Summary of Christian Doctrine*, 31.

15. J. I. Packer, *Concise Theology* (Wheaton, IL: Tyndale, 1993), 28.

16. Ibid., 35.

17. Berkhof, *A Summary of Christian Doctrine*, 32.

18. Packer, *Concise Theology*, 31.

19. Ibid.

20. Philip Bennett Power, *The "I Wills" of the Psalms* (Carlisle, PA: The Banner of Truth Trust, 1985), 2.

Chapter 4

1. Mark Galli and Ted Olsen, eds., *131 Christians Everyone Should Know* (Nashville, TN: Broadman and Holman, 2000), 248.

2. Ibid.

3. J. D. Douglas, *Who's Who in Christian History* (Wheaton, IL: Tyndale, 1992), 427.

4. http://www.wholesomewords.org/missions/bliving5.html.

5. Rob Mackenzie, *David Livingstone: The Truth Behind the Legend* (Ross-Shire, Scotland: Christian Focus, 1993), 25–26.

6. Phillip Keller, cited by James Montgomery Boice, *Joshua: An Expositional Commentary* (Grand Rapids, MI: Baker, 1989), 178.

7. Herbert Lockyer, *All the Men of the Bible* (Grand Rapids, MI: Zondervan, 1958), 206.

8. http://online.wsj.com/article/SB121556087828237463.html?mod=opinion_main_commentaries.

9. Daniel Yergin, *The Prize: The Epic Quest for Oil, Money and Power* (New York: Free, 1993), 11–12.

10. Ibid., 15.

11. D. Martyn Lloyd-Jones, *The Christian Soldier: An Exposition of Ephesians 6:10–20* (Grand Rapids, MI: Baker, 1977), 17.

12. George Müller, *Autobiography of George Müller*, compiled by G. Fred Bergin (Denton, TX: Westminster Literature Resources, 2003), 386–87.

13. Oswald Sanders, *Promised Land Living* (Chicago: Moody, 1984), 36.

14. John J. Murray, *Behind a Frowning Providence* (Carlisle, PA: The Banner of Truth Trust, 1990), 16–17.

15. J. I. Packer, *Faithfulness and Holiness: The Witness of J. C. Ryle* (Wheaton, IL: Crossway, 2002), 22.

16. http://www.biblebb.com/files/ryle/j_c_ryle.htm.

17. Packer, *Faithfulness and Holiness* (Wheaton, IL: Crossway, 2002), 25.

18. Ibid., 26.

Chapter 5

1. http://www.britainexpress.com/History/bio/pugin.htm.

2. Paul Johnson, *Creators* (New York: HarperCollins, 2006), 138.

3. http://www.amazon.com/Brokenness-How-Redeems-Pain-Suffering/dp/0976377004.

4. Lon Solomon, *Brokenness* (Potomac, MD: Red Door, 2005), 40–41.

5. Ronald F. Youngblood, ed., *Nelson's New Illustrated Bible Dictionary* (Nashville, TN: Thomas Nelson, 1995), 491.

6. F. W. Boreham, cited by Warren Wiersbe, *The Bible Exposition Commentary: History* (Colorado Springs, CO: Victor/David C. Cook, 2003), 381.

7. Thomas Watson, *All Things for Good* (Carlisle, PA: The Banner of Truth Trust, 1663), 28.

8. Nancy K. Frankenberry, *The Faith of Scientists in Their Own Words* (Princeton, NJ: Princeton University, 2008), 123.

9. Randal Keynes, *Darwin, His Daughter, and Human Evolution* (New York: Riverhead, 2001), inside cover flap.

10. George M. Marsden, *Jonathan Edwards: A Life* (New Haven, CT: Yale University, 2003), 63.

11. John Piper, *Desiring God* (Portland, OR: Multnomah, 1986), 29.

12. Ibid. 63.

13. http://books.google.com/books?id=eIQYwBjfJ5AC&pg=PA319&lpg=PA319&dq=da rwin+loss+of+taste&source=web&ots=YXtk2gXr1T&sig=1QdDNrfi3GF9PvmO4exFS m2NZzc&hl=en&sa=X&oi=book_result&resnum=10&ct=result.

14. http://www.britainexpress.com/History/bio/pugin.htm.

Chapter 6

1. Nate Miller, "My Flight Crashed in My Own Front Yard," *Financial Times*, October 5, 2008, Life & Arts.

2. http://infomotions.com/etexts/gutenberg/dirs/etext06/7bees10.htm.

3. Phillip W. Keller, *Lessons from a Sheep Dog* (Nashville, TN: W Publishing, 2002), vii–viii.

4. http://www.puritansermons.com/newton/Newt_j1.htm.

5. Keller, *Lessons from a Sheep Dog*, xvi–xvii.

6. J. Robert Clinton, *The Making of a Leader* (Colorado Springs, CO: NavPress, 1988), back cover.

7. Ibid., 46.

8. Ibid.

9. Richard Brookhiser, *George Washington on Leadership* (New York: Basic, 2008), 31.

10. Ibid., 33–34.

11. William Bridges, *Transitions* (Reading, MA: Perseus, 1980), back cover.

Chapter 7

1. LTG (Ret.) William G. Boykin, *Never Surrender* (New York: Faith Words, 2008), 78.

2. Phillip Keller, *Joshua: Mighty Warrior and Man of Faith* (Grand Rapids, MI: Kregel, 1983), 46.

3. Ronald F. Youngblood, *Nelson's New Illustrated Bible Dictionary* (Nashville, TN: Thomas Nelson, 1995), 706.

4. Cleon L. Rogers, Jr. and Cleon L. Rogers III, *The New Linguistic and Exegetical Key to the Greek New Testament* (Grand Rapids, MI: Zondervan, 1998), 402.

5. Boykin, *Never Surrender*, 89.

6. Rogers, *New Linguistic*, 449, 560.

7. http://en.wikipedia.org/wiki/Philippe_Petit.

8. http://www.guardian.co.uk/theobserver/2003/jan/19/features.magazine57.

9. Boykin, *Never Surrender*, 71.

10. F. B. Meyer, *Great Men of the Bible, Volume 1* (Grand Rapids, MI: Zondervan, 1981), 220.

11. Boykin, *Never Surrender*, 76.

12. Warren Wiersbe, *The Bible Exposition Commentary: History* (Colorado Springs, CO: Victor/David C. Cook, 2003), 19.

Chapter 8

1. http://survivethemeltdown.org/.

2. www.maninthemirror.org.

3. Patrick M. Morley, *The Man in the Mirror* (Brentwood, TN: Wolgemuth & Hyatt, 1989), 74.

4. Genesis 50:20.

5. I am indebted to Robert J. Morgan and his wonderful book *Red Sea Rules* for this insight.

6. C. F. Keil and F. Delitzsch, *Commentary on the Old Testament in Ten Volumes, Volume 2* (Grand Rapids, MI: William B. Eerdmans, 1980), 45.

Chapter 9

1. Harvey C. Mansfield, *Manliness* (New Haven, CT: Yale University, 2006).

2. Ibid., 18.

3. *Financial Times*, October 5, 2008, Life & Arts, 15.

4. See 1 Peter 5:8.

5. Paul P. Enns, *Joshua: Bible Study Commentary* (Grand Rapids, MI: Zondervan, 1981), 36.

6. http://www.masshist.org/adams/quotes.cfm.

Chapter 10

1. Paul Johnson, "Let Economies Cure Themselves," *Forbes Magazine*, September 1, 2008, 27.

2. J. D. Douglas, ed., *The New International Dictionary of the Christian Church* (Grand Rapids, MI: Zondervan, 1974), 733.

3. Ronald F. Youngblood, ed., *Nelson's New Illustrated Bible Dictionary* (Nashville, TN: Thomas Nelson, 1986), 278.

4. There is an account in Genesis 34 of Dinah, the daughter of Jacob and Leah, who was raped by the son of the Shechemite king. The king attempted to make things right, and it was agreed that the son would marry the girl. Two of Dinah's brothers insisted that all of the Shechemite men must be circumcised before they would enter into a covenant with them. The Shechemites agreed and three days after their circumcision, "when they were sore," two of the brothers, Simeon and Levi, took their swords and slaughtered every man (Gen. 34:25). The men were completely vulnerable and unable to defend themselves.

5. John F. Walvoord and Roy B. Zuck, *The Bible Knowledge Commentary* (Wheaton, IL: Victor, 1985), 337.

6. D. Martyn Lloyd-Jones, *Studies in the Sermon on the Mount* (Grand Rapids, MI: Wm. B. Eerdmans, 1974), 157.

7. George Müller, *Autobiography of George Müller* (Denton, TX: Westminster Literature Resources, 2003), publisher's preface.

8. Ibid., introduction.

9. James Montgomery Boice, *Joshua: An Expositional Commentary* (Grand Rapids, MI: Baker, 1989), 9–10.

Chapter 11

1. http://www.starwars.com/databank/location/deathstar/.

2. Paul P. Enns, *Joshua: A Bible Study Commentary* (Grand Rapids, MI: Zondervan, 1981), 55.

3. Leon Wood, *A Survey of Israel's History* (Grand Rapids, MI: Zondervan, 1970), 174.

4. Merrill F. Unger, cited by Enns, *Joshua,* 57.

5. Martyn Lloyd-Jones, *The Christian Warfare* (Grand Rapids, MI: Baker, 1976), 313.

6. http://www.aviation-history.com/airmen/boyd.htm.

7. http://www.americanthinker.com/2008/08/mccain_and_the_ooda_loop.html.

8. Other than a glancing reference to them in a passage about Rahab, Hebrews 11:31.

9. http://www.informz.net/pfm/archives/archive_647715.html.

Chapter 12

1. Paul Johnson, "In Business, Simplicity Is Golden," *Forbes Magazine*, March 16, 2009, 17.

2. C. Stacey Woods, *Some Ways of God* (Downers Grove, IL: InterVarsity, 1975), 15.

3. Franklin Graham, *Rebel with a Cause* (Nashville, TN: Thomas Nelson, 1995), 97–98.

4. Basil Miller, *George Müller: Man of Faith and Miracles* (Minneapolis, MN: Bethany, 1972), 18, 36.

5. Andree Seu, "Way Out on a Limb," *World Magazine*, January 17, 2009, 79.

6. George Müller, *Autobiography of George Müller* (Denton, TX: Westminster Christian Resources, 2003), viii.